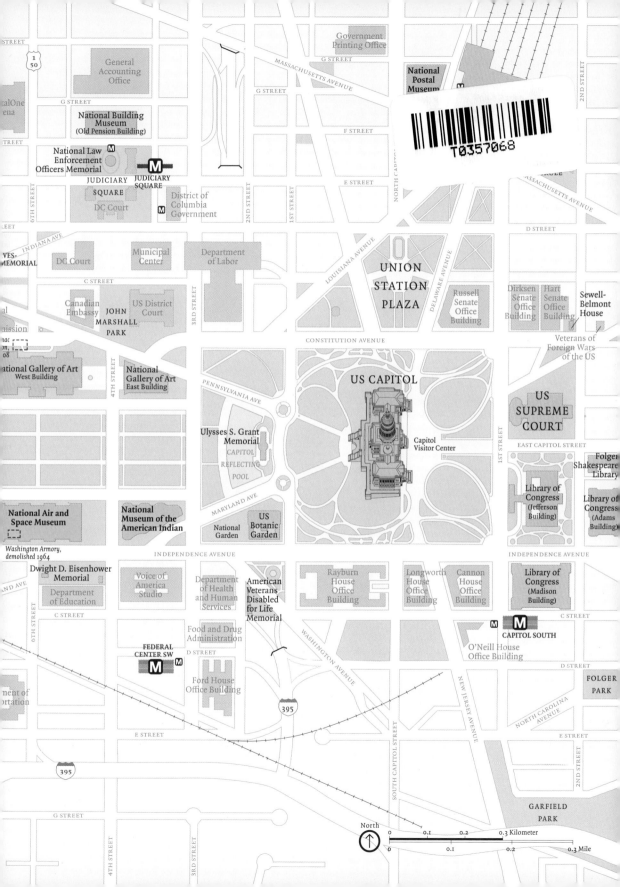

A GUIDE TO SMITHSONIAN
ARCHITECTURE

Heather Ewing and Amy Ballard · Smithsonian Books · Washington, DC

Second Edition

Funding for this book was provided by the
Smithsonian Women's Committee and the
Office of Planning, Design and Construction,
Smithsonian Facilities.

Prepared in collaboration with the
Office of Architectural History and Historic
Preservation, Smithsonian Institution.

Edited by Joanne Reams

Previous edition edited by Diane Maddex

Designed by Robert L. Wiser

Library of Congress
Cataloging-in-Publication Data

Names: Ewing, Heather P., author. |
Ballard, Amy, author.
Title: A guide to Smithsonian architecture /
Heather Ewing and Amy Ballard.

Description: Second edition. |
Washington, DC : Smithsonian Books, [2022] |
Includes bibliographical references and index.
Identifiers: LCCN 2021041631 |
ISBN 9781588347176 (paperback)
Subjects: LCSH: Smithsonian Institution—
Buildings. | Museum buildings—United
States. | Research institutes—United States. |
Architecture—United States.
Classification: LCC NA6751 .E95 2022 |
DDC 727/.60009753—dc23
LC record available at
https://lccn.loc.gov/2021041631

Second Edition

26 25 24 23 22   5 4 3 2 1

Printed in China

All illustrations in this book are from the
collections of the Smithsonian Institution,
except for the following:

Endpapers: Peter Penczer and the National
Park Service; pages 8–9, 79, 100, 102:
© Eduard Hueber, 2008/archphoto.com; pages
15 top, 18, 24, 27 top: National Archives;
page 30: Bettman/Corbis; page 37: Richard E.
Stamm; pages 41, 47 bottom, 90, 91: Ron
Blunt; page 53: James W. Gleason; page 56:
Chun-Hsi Wong; page 93: Susana Raab;
page 103: © 2021 Juan Muñoz Estate, Artists
Rights Society (ARS), NY/VEGAP, Madrid;
page 107: Quinn Evans; pages 134–35, 142
bottom, 143–49: Alan Karchmer; page 155:
EwingCole; page 157: Bjarke Ingels Group.

Most of the contemporary photographs
were taken by Smithsonian photographers.
Please see the acknowledgments on page 162
for a complete list.

Endpapers: Map of the National Mall,
showing many of the Smithsonian's museums
and other national landmarks.

Page 1: An 1893 mosaic of the Smithsonian
seal, by Augustus Saint-Gaudens, located at
the entrance to the Regents' Room in the Castle.

Pages 2–3: The final stone of the National
Museum of Natural History's south portico
being laid on May 11, 1909.

Page 4: The International Exchange Service,
one of the Smithsonian's earliest departments,
which promoted the institution's scholarly
publications. The staff, posing in front of the
east entrance in 1891, included Solomon
Brown (seated at left front, in a bowler hat),
the first African American employee, who
worked at the Smithsonian for fifty-four
years, and Mazie R. Fountaine, a clerk
(standing, in a white dress).

Page 168: James Smithson's neoclassical
marble sarcophagus, made in Genoa,
Italy. Located in the Castle crypt, it is
embellished with funerary ornamentation,
such as the pine-cone finial at the top,
symbolizing regeneration.

Contents

FOREWORD

Much of the way I think about architecture was shaped by my time spent in Chicago, surrounded by signature buildings designed by giants like Louis Sullivan, Ludwig Mies van der Rohe, and Frank Lloyd Wright. They helped inspire me when I returned to the nation's capital, tasked with the daunting goal of making the National Museum of African American History and Culture a reality.

The African American museum is our newest building, but the design of each Smithsonian museum is a snapshot in time, reflecting styles, representing values, and relaying a history lesson about the era in which it was built. All our museums have fascinating stories within their bricks, cement, and steel—as do the ingenuity, challenges, and perseverance that accompanied their creation.

Luckily, we were able to enlist Heather Ewing and Amy Ballard to update these stories for the new edition of *A Guide to Smithsonian Architecture*. It is not the only contribution to the Smithsonian for which they are acclaimed; a gifted research associate at Smithsonian Libraries and Archives, Heather literally wrote the book on our founder, *The Lost World of James Smithson*, and Amy retired as senior historic preservation specialist emerita after a distinguished forty-year career at the Smithsonian.

As someone who has worked in four different Smithsonian buildings during my career, this guide has given me an even greater appreciation for the places that have enabled my work and that of my colleagues. As a historian, I am impressed by how impeccably researched this book is, giving unique insight into the way these buildings came about and how their forms follow their various functions. I am confident it will do the same for anyone interested in architecture or the history of the Smithsonian, inspiring extra appreciation for our 175-year-old institution.

Looking ahead, we will have to see if Heather and Amy are available to work on another revision. The congressional approval of the Smithsonian American Women's History Museum and the National Museum of the American Latino means that two new additions should be joining the Smithsonian family, each with new creation stories to tell. Until then, this is the authoritative guide to our architectural legacy, giving the rich history of our museums equal billing to the treasures, scholarship, programming, and research contained within.

Lonnie G. Bunch III
Secretary of the Smithsonian Institution

In the late nineteenth century, the Castle's north carriage porch or porte-cochere (opposite) looked out onto the picturesque, winding paths of the Smithsonian Park. The 1901 McMillan Plan, inspired by the city plan designed by Pierre Charles L'Enfant in 1791, turned this area into the classical, open greensward that we recognize today.

Pages 8–9: Today the National Mall is lined with museums, as envisioned by the McMillan Plan. The red sandstone towers of the Castle and the Beaux-Arts dome of the Natural History Museum emerge from the trees in this view from the foot of Capitol Hill.

Preface

The Largest Collection

The Largest Collection

Many visitors to Washington, DC, think that most, if not all, of the Smithsonian museums are located on the National Mall and downtown. But there is much more to the Smithsonian than its buildings in the heart of the capital. On a daily basis, the institution actually takes care of more than 650 properties—covering nearly fourteen million square feet of buildings—in locations from nearby Maryland and Virginia to New York City, Massachusetts, and Florida, and farther afield to Arizona, Hawaii, Belize, Panama, and more.

The stewardship of what can be called the Smithsonian's largest collection—its buildings—has been an ongoing concern since the first section of its first building, now known as the Castle, opened in 1849. However, it was not until 1880 that the institution's first superintendent of buildings, Henry Horan, was named. He held the post until 1896, when the Division of Buildings and Superintendence was created. With the Smithsonian's growth, this division has undergone several name changes and reorganizations. Now Smithsonian Facilities, it is responsible for the daily care and maintenance of the institution's buildings and grounds. Under its umbrella are most of the institution's support services: safety, health and environmental management, facilities management (maintenance), geospatial, horticulture, project management, master planning, architectural history and historic preservation, real estate, design, and engineering and construction. Its staff of more than 1,100 employees works mostly behind the scenes to protect, maintain, and curate the Smithsonian's architectural heritage.

In addition to encompassing and exhibiting the collections, the buildings of the Smithsonian themselves serve as cultural icons. Their forms illustrate changing styles and sensibilities over the course of the last two centuries. Each one tells a story. The mid-nineteenth-century turreted Castle was a bold, eclectic manifestation of the Smithsonian's mission of increase and diffusion; the imposing classicism of the domed National Museum of Natural History reflects the grand national ambitions of the turn of the twentieth century; and the glass-filled National Air and Space Museum of the 1970s adopts a spare modernism to bring the exuberance of the space age to the Mall. In the twenty-first century, two extraordinary landmark buildings, the National Museum of the American Indian and the National Museum of African American History and Culture, have greatly expanded the aesthetic language of the Mall, reflecting their missions to enlarge our understanding of the vastness and complexity of the American story.

Many of the Smithsonian's buildings are National Historic Landmarks or are included in the National Register of Historic Places, the official roster of the nation's historic properties, sites, districts, structures, objects, and landmarks. More than eighty thousand sites in the United States are listed in the National Register, and 2,400 are National Historic Landmarks. The institution is proud that several of its buildings carry these designations, which are deemed by the secretary of the interior to have exceptional value to the nation.

In 1993 the Architectural History and Historic Preservation Office developed a historic preservation policy for the Smithsonian, outlining the institution's commitment to protect and preserve the buildings and sites in its care. Every design and construction project initiated by the institution follows recommended guidelines entitled the Secretary of the Interior's Standards and Guidelines for the Treatment of Historic Properties. Public and private owners of historic properties use these standards throughout the United States to ensure sound preservation methodology for projects large and small.

This guide presents the Smithsonian's buildings in the order in which they were built or acquired by the institution, beginning with the Castle and ending with the National Museum of African American History and Culture. When a site includes distinct but intertwined facilities, all are discussed together under the main museum listing. At the end of the book are grouped less visible but no less important structures, the institution's research centers and support facilities. For readers interested in a strictly architectural chronology of the Smithsonian's buildings, which actually begins with Robert Mills's Patent Office Building of 1836 (today the home of the Smithsonian American Art Museum and the National Portrait Gallery), there is a chronology at the back of the book.

In 1964, shortly after becoming the Smithsonian's eighth secretary, S. Dillon Ripley observed that "the facilities and resources at the Smithsonian are tremendous . . . yet with the phenomenal growth of the Smithsonian have come almost awe-inspiring opportunities and challenges." These words hold true today and no doubt will in the future, as the Smithsonian embarks on the creation of two new museums, the Smithsonian American Women's History Museum and the National Museum of the American Latino, and continues to care for its architectural legacy. Although the Smithsonian is the caretaker of these buildings, it holds them in trust on your behalf. Enjoy!

Heather Ewing and Amy Ballard

Pages 12–13: James Renwick designed the Castle in a Norman Romanesque style, inspired by the medieval architecture of English universities. The west end of the building, with its rose window, resembles a chapel.

INTRODUCTION

An 1881 engraving of James Smithson, who bequeathed his estate to establish the Smithsonian Institution, is based on a miniature by Henri Johns (painted in France in 1816).

"The name of Smithson is not to be transmitted to posterity by a monument of brick and mortar, but by the effects of his institution on his fellow men." So wrote Joseph Henry (1797–1878), the first secretary of the Smithsonian, a month after Congress passed the legislation establishing the Smithsonian Institution in August 1846. There had been much debate over the bequest of James Smithson (ca. 1765–1829), which called for the creation in Washington of "an establishment for the increase and diffusion of knowledge among men." Some wondered why an English scientist who had never set foot in the United States would leave it his fortune (more than a half million dollars in the 1830s), and many questioned what exactly an institution for the increase and diffusion of knowledge should be—a national library, a university, a museum, an astrophysical observatory, a teacher training college? The act of Congress included a little bit of everything, and some members of the Board of Regents, the governing body for the new Smithsonian, believed that a grand and symbolic building to house all of these functions would establish the new institution's place in the nation's capital.

Joseph Henry, America's foremost scientist in the mid-nineteenth century, thought instead that Smithson's extraordinary gift should be devoted to original scientific research. He saw in the idea of the Smithsonian the opportunity to place the United States on a scientific footing equal to that of Europe. The way to perpetuate Smithson's name, Henry reasoned, was to build a community of scientists, support their work, and disseminate their discoveries through a system of publications. In fact, his vision did become a reality. The scientific work of the Smithsonian, although little known to the public, is a critically important part of its mission. Today the institution runs scientific stations and research programs around the world, including a global volcanism project and a migratory bird study, astrophysical observatories from Cambridge, Massachusetts, to Chile, and laboratories in the tropical forest of Panama. The Smithsonian's longstanding support of basic research has stimulated the development of many practical advances. Its funding of an unknown college professor named Robert Goddard in the early twentieth century led to the discovery of the principles of rocket propulsion and launched the space age; Margaret Geller's studies at the Smithsonian Astrophysical Observatory of the spatial distribution of galaxies have given humanity a new understanding of the structure of the universe; leadership in the field of captive breeding at the National Zoo and Conservation Biology Institute has led to international collaborations to support the reintroduction of critically endangered or extinct-in-the-wild species such as the golden lion tamarin, the Guam rail, and the scimitar-horned oryx; and the Federal Bureau of Investigation's frequent calls

on the Natural History Museum's expert anthropologists and their encyclopedic collections led to the founding of the field of forensic analysis. Through this work, the impact of Smithson's name on society has been immense.

But Henry was certainly mistaken about the dangers of architectural showpieces. The castellated Smithsonian building he opposed so vigorously has become the iconic symbol of the institution and an architectural landmark. It was joined in subsequent decades by numerous other significant buildings designed expressly for the Smithsonian by major architects, such as Charles A. Platt, Gordon Bunshaft, Gyo Obata, and Sir David Adjaye. In the breadth of all the Smithsonian buildings, including those acquired over time—among them one of the nation's finest Greek Revival public buildings—can be seen a microcosm of the history of American architecture. This book offers an introduction to the Smithsonian's architecture as it explores how the Smithsonian has grown over the course of its 175-year history, beginning with the Castle and carrying through to the National Museum of African American History and Culture.

When the Castle was completed in 1855, it became the first public building on the Mall. This image by famed Civil War photographer Mathew Brady shows it rising above the tree-lined Smithsonian Park. At the time the US Capitol dome was still under construction.

Joseph Henry and his family lived for many years in the Castle's east wing. In 1862 they were photographed on the Smithsonian grounds near their home by the American artist and scientist Titian Ramsay Peale.

Above the north entrance of the Arts and Industries Building is a plaque reading "National Museum, 1879," reflecting the building's original purpose. Its polychrome brick decoration and exhuberant design were inspired by world's fair exposition architecture.

The Smithsonian's founding act made it the national repository for the collections of the United States, and the development of its buildings is inextricably tied to the history and the growth of these collections. Government expeditions formed to chart and study the American West included scientists who sent tens of thousands of specimens back to Washington. The first Smithsonian building, the red sandstone Castle, rapidly filled with artifacts and specimens (and with the young men who studied and catalogued them, while living in the little rooms high in the Castle's towers). It housed ethnographic and archeological collections, minerals and meteorites, dinosaurs, historic relics, botanical and natural history specimens, and paintings and sculpture.

The Philadelphia Centennial Exhibition of 1876, for which the Smithsonian was charged with preparing all the government's exhibits, celebrated the nation's emerging economic and industrial strength. The history of technology soon became one of the institution's more prominent fields of collecting. With the influx of material that came to Washington after the fair, the need for a new building became overwhelming. Congress responded, and the exuberant polychrome brick building now known as Arts and Industries was begun in 1879 and completed two years later. It was the first building dedicated entirely to the US National Museum, cementing the Smithsonian's role as curator of the national collections. Over the course of the next half century, the institution was a significant presence at many expositions and world's fairs—which in turn ensured that the collections continued to expand exponentially.

Surrounded by specimens, curators in ethnology at the turn of the twentieth century work in the Arts and Industries Building on a newly installed balcony—added to accommodate the burgeoning collections.

Within a few years of the completion of the Arts and Industries Building, the need was clearly apparent for yet more space, in particular room for storage and curatorial work. The Smithsonian began to appeal to Congress as early as 1885, pleas that continued on a regular basis until construction started in 1903 on a new building for the National Museum (the Natural History Museum, across the Mall from the Castle). Separate facilities for research work began in the 1890s, with the construction of a utilitarian wooden shed for the Astrophysical Observatory in the South Yard behind the Castle.

The story of the growth of the Smithsonian and its collections is entwined with the development of the National Mall. Congress allocated the Smithsonian a fifty-acre plot, between Seventh and Twelfth Streets, as part of its original establishment. These grounds were landscaped in a romantic style by Andrew Jackson Downing (1815–52) in the early 1850s, with heavily wooded areas and curving carriage paths. As the Smithsonian expanded, its new museum buildings—Arts and Industries,

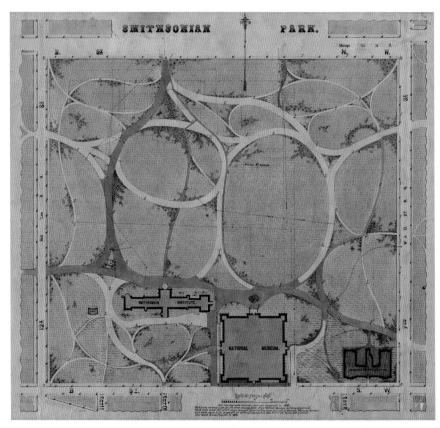

An 1882 plan for the grounds of the Smithsonian shows the romantic nature of the park before the McMillan Commission of 1901 reshaped the Mall as it appears today. The buildings shown are the long, narrow Castle, the square Arts and Industries Building, and the E-shaped Army Medical Museum. Adolf Cluss designed both the Arts and Industries Building and the Medical Museum. The tiny square to the left of the Castle was the Laboratory of Natural History, where taxidermists and the institution's photographer worked.

Natural History, and the Freer—were all built within the original bounds of
this Smithsonian Park. During the second half of the nineteenth century, these
grounds remained quite distinct from the rest of the area now known as the
Mall, which included the Agriculture Department, with its botanical gardens;
the Armory, with its supporting buildings; and even the Baltimore and Potomac
train station, whose rail line cut across the Mall and its park areas.

When the McMillan Commission undertook to create a Beaux-Arts style for
Washington in 1901, it focused on turning the Victorian Mall into a grand neoclassical greensward reminiscent of Pierre Charles L'Enfant's original eighteenth-
century vision for the capital. The Capitol and the Washington Monument
were to be linked in one ensemble, creating an architectural stage set that mani-
fested the political ideals of the rapidly expanding nation. The great open space
of the newly designed Mall between these public monuments would, according
to the commission, afford "spacious sites for buildings devoted to scientific
purposes and to the great museums." The Smithsonian's Natural History
Museum, with its imposing classical portico and Roman dome, became a model
for the new classical architecture that was to define the city's monumental core.
In its large-scale classical massing and its careful siting on the north side of
the Mall, Natural History set a precedent for the museums that would follow.

*The Natural History Museum,
seen here under construction
in 1909, was the first museum
building on the Mall to follow
the stylistic ideals set out by
the McMillan Plan.*

The Small Mammal House, shown soon after its completion in 1906, is now the oldest building at the National Zoo. Known today as the Think Tank, it was designed by Hornblower and Marshall, the architects of the Natural History Museum.

The expansion of the Smithsonian at the outset of the twentieth century was driven in large part by the acquisition of new collections—items that resulted from the pursuit of different aspects of the original congressional charter. Although a "gallery of art" had been included in the 1846 act and existed in the Castle at the time of its completion in 1855, it was not really until the turn of the next century, under the third secretary, Samuel P. Langley (1834–1906), that the Smithsonian began to focus on collecting art. In 1906 Harriet Lane Johnston, the niece and White House hostess of President James Buchanan, donated a number of paintings, which formed the nucleus of the original National Gallery of Art, founded under the Smithsonian's auspices. (Later it became the National Collection of Fine Arts and today is the Smithsonian American Art Museum.) This was followed by the donation of Charles Lang Freer's collection of Asian art and the funds to build the Freer Gallery, the first Smithsonian museum dedicated exclusively to the fine arts. Freer's gift to the nation continued a tradition of philanthropy started by none other than Smithson himself; it was echoed later in the century by Joseph Hirshhorn, who donated his modern art and sculpture collections and the ring-shaped building and garden to house it. This tradition of the capitalist-turned-benefactor—a distinctly American phenomenon—is also an important element of the Smithsonian story and the development of its buildings.

The Smithsonian's architecture reflects the acquisition and the growth of the collections, but it also reveals a changing understanding of museology, of how to present objects to the public, and of how to care for and curate them. This relationship is perhaps nowhere more evident than in the Smithsonian's National Zoo. The zoo's oldest extant building, the original Small Mammal House of 1906 (today called the Think Tank), is a typical nineteenth-century menagerie building; it stands in stark contrast to the barless moat design of the nearby Lion and Tiger House of the 1970s or the Elephant Trails project of the early 2010s, which overhauled the elephant habitat to permit the animals to live and roam in a herd. In the case of the US National Museum, the initial exhibits were accommodated within the linear plan of the Castle building. George Brown Goode, an early curator, did pioneering work in museum studies using the flexible square plan of the Arts and Industries Building as his laboratory. In terms of floor plan and exhibition display, the leap from the Castle to Arts and Industries was a large one, but the jump from the open-plan pavilions of Arts and Industries to the monumental halls of the Natural History Museum was even greater. Both the Castle and Arts and Industries "furnished many valuable object lessons," explained Smithsonian leaders at the completion of the new Natural History building, "teaching perhaps more what to avoid than what to retain, and in the prolonged effort to adapt them to the storage and exhibition of the constantly overflowing collections it was but natural that very definite opinions should have been reached as to the general and detailed requirements of a modern museum."

The idea of what constituted a modern museum had changed a great deal by the 1964 opening of the Museum of History and Technology, as the National Museum of American History was originally known. Likewise born of a reevaluation of the best means to display collections and educate and engage visitors, it was the culmination of a program of exhibition modernization that the Smithsonian undertook in the 1950s. Key leaders of this charge were Secretary Leonard Carmichael (1898–1973) and the curator who became the founding director of the Museum of History and Technology, Frank Taylor. The advances of that age—the replacement of glass-fronted cases with large built-out dioramas, which created contained environments but obscured a building's original features—were eventually undone nearly half a century later; examples can be seen in the Kenneth E. Behring Family Hall of Mammals, the Sant Ocean Hall, and the new David H. Koch Hall of Fossils—Deep Time in the Natural History Museum.

The Museum of History and Technology (today the National Museum of American History), completed in 1964, introduced a modernist interpretation of the classical language that dominated public buildings in DC for so many decades. The recessed bays, here illuminated at night, created an effect that subtly recalled the colonnaded Lincoln Memorial at the west end of the Mall.

The Hirshhorn Museum surrounds a courtyard enlivened by a central fountain. Nearly all the windows of the museum face this protected space.

The modernization campaign at midcentury heralded a period of tremendous growth for the Smithsonian, especially in the arts. The National Museum of American History, when it opened in 1964, was the first new Smithsonian building on the Mall since the Freer in 1923. Despite its sleek modernity, it marked the continuation of the McMillan Plan's vision of a National Mall lined with monumental, classically inspired museums. It was followed by the Hirshhorn Museum and Sculpture Garden and the National Air and Space Museum, further modernist variations on this theme. From four buildings on the Mall for much of the first half of the twentieth century, the Smithsonian counted ten there as the twenty-first century dawned.

In 1959 the Army presented the Smithsonian with a full-scale Jupiter-C missile, topped by an example of the eighty-inch Explorer I satellite the rocket had launched into space. The only place large enough to display the growing space collection was on the west side of the Arts and Industries Building, which became known as Rocket Row.

During the 1960s and 1970s, the Smithsonian became a leader in the adaptation and reuse of historic buildings. Of the new museums to join the Smithsonian collection then, many of them were housed in historic structures. The National Collection of Fine Arts (now the Smithsonian American Art Museum) and the National Portrait Gallery opened in the Old Patent Office Building, one of the most important buildings of early Washington. The Renwick Gallery of Art, dedicated to American crafts and decorative arts, brought life back to the original Corcoran Gallery of Art, an exquisite example of the French Second Empire style designed by James Renwick Jr., architect of the original Smithsonian Castle. The Cooper Hewitt Smithsonian Design Museum took over Andrew Carnegie's Gilded Age mansion in New York City, preserving both building and collection. The Old Patent Office Building and the Renwick had each been used for decades as offices, and the Carnegie Mansion as a school; reuse ensured their restoration as well as public access.

During the Civil War, the museum building that became the Renwick Gallery of Art served as offices for the quartermaster general, Montgomery C. Meigs. The 1824 house to the right is now part of Blair House, the presidential guest complex.

The Old Patent Office Building was adapted for use as the Smithsonian American Art Museum and the National Portrait Gallery. The original Model Hall (above) once displayed the working models that inventors submitted along with their patent applications. Today it houses the Smithsonian American Art Museum's Luce Foundation Center, a visible-art storage and study center.

Modern art has been exhibited in the Smithsonian American Art Museum's Lincoln Gallery since 1968. Abraham Lincoln held his second inaugural ball in this columned space.

A variety of African sources inspired the architecture of the Anacostia Community Museum. Patterned red brick walls evoke woven Kente cloth, while cylinders with diamonds of glass block and blue tile reference the remarkable ruins of the medieval sub-Saharan city of Great Zimbabwe.

This period of expansion at the Smithsonian mirrored a time of social change in the United States, an era when the civil rights and women's movements were bringing new perspectives to the telling and exploration of American history. The institution committed to reaching underserved constituencies, opening the Anacostia Neighborhood Museum in 1967 in the predominantly African American neighborhood of Anacostia in southeast DC. It was an experiment to take the Smithsonian off the Mall—in the words of Secretary S. Dillon Ripley (1913–2001), to make it a less forbidding collection of marble halls. The Smithsonian's growth at this time also acquired an increasingly global outlook, as the institution saw itself in dialogue with the larger world, Africa and Asia in particular. The Folklife Festival, celebrating living and intangible cultural heritage traditions from around the world, was inaugurated on the Mall in 1967. As part of a Festival of India, the Natural History Museum hosted *Aditi: The Living Arts of India* in 1985, and in 1986 the Renwick Gallery showcased a major Russian art exhibition, with rarely loaned works from the Soviet Union. The Smithsonian worked with Ghana in the early 1990s on revitalizing the Cape Coast Castle Museum, a cultural project located in one of approximately forty "slave castles" built by European traders on the west coast of Africa and site of the infamous "door of no return."

Charles Lindbergh flies the Spirit of St. Louis over Gatun Lake in the Panama Canal Zone in 1928 (above). The first home of the Smithsonian's Tropical Research Institute was on Barro Colorado Island, in the middle of the lake. Lindbergh's plane now resides at the Air and Space Museum.

In 1950, Barro Colorado Island was dotted with structures built to support Smithsonian scientists (left). A small rail brought supplies up from the dock to the main building.

The construction of the Quadrangle complex in the 1980s posed many challenges, as it was located below the water table and adjacent to three of the Smithsonian's historic structures.

This global outlook led ultimately to the creation of the Quadrangle in 1987, which encompasses the Arthur M. Sackler Gallery (which today, together with the Freer Gallery of Art, forms the Smithsonian's National Museum of Asian Art), the National Museum of African Art, the S. Dillon Ripley Center, and the Enid A. Haupt Garden. It was "time to look beyond our immediate horizon," said Ripley, who considered the Quadrangle one of the most significant projects of his Smithsonian career. The Quadrangle was also a clever rethinking of the South Yard behind the Castle, which had spawned so many Smithsonian initiatives—from the taxidermy sheds where exhibit preparation for the world's fairs took place, to the animal enclosures that led to the National Zoo, to the observatory shed that formed the embryonic Astrophysical Observatory, to the Quonset hut that housed the first National Air Museum. This area, once dedicated to behind-the-scenes work, is now a public showcase.

The more recent growth of the Smithsonian has focused on expanding the narrative and understanding of the American experience and displaying it in all its diversity. In 1997 the Smithsonian Latino Center was created to celebrate Latino contributions to American heritage and culture, and the Asian Pacific American Center was established the following year. The National Museum of the American Indian was developed as a living museum, in consultation with tribes across this hemisphere; it remains dedicated to serving as a thoughtful and

honest partner and conduit to Native cultures past and present. The National Museum of African American History and Culture opened in a stunning, award-winning building adjacent to the Washington Monument in 2016; it explores the American story through the lens of Black history and culture. And in 2020, Congress approved the creation of two new Smithsonian museums: the National Museum of the American Latino and the American Women's History Museum.

The Sackler Gallery's pyramidal roofs were designed to complement the Smithsonian's Arts and Industries Building, while its color was inspired by the nearby Freer Gallery of Art.

One hundred and seventy-five years after the establishment of the Smithsonian, the institution comprises—perhaps to what would be Joseph Henry's chagrin—an extraordinary collection of bricks and mortar. It has grown to become the largest museum and research complex in the world, engaged in work in many parts of the globe as well as out in space. The place today no doubt would exceed James Smithson's wildest dreams. And yet at its core, it remains true to his grandest ideals: along the National Mall in Washington, DC, on what is arguably one of the country's most important and symbolic public spaces, are buildings and collections dedicated to the "increase and diffusion of knowledge" that are free and open to all.

THE CASTLE

The turreted red sandstone Castle building, a landmark of American architecture, has been the symbol of the Smithsonian for more than 150 years. Before it was built, Washington, DC, was a city of monumental neoclassical buildings: the White House, the Capitol, the Treasury Building, and the Old Patent Office Building (which today houses the Smithsonian American Art Museum and the National Portrait Gallery). The arrival of the Smithsonian's first building, with its dark stone, nine asymmetrical towers, and its fortress-like embattlements, represented a powerful departure from this classicism and marked the introduction of picturesque styles in American public architecture.

This 1860 engraving is one of the few known images of James Renwick Jr., who was only twenty-eight years old when he won the competition to design the Castle. He was also the architect of the building that became the Renwick Gallery of Art.

The choice of a medieval revival style for the Smithsonian building was deliberate. Although the classical models that dominated Washington's public buildings evoked ancient Greece and Rome, the Castle's Romanesque form allied the building symbolically with historic English collegiate architecture, like that of Oxford and Cambridge. Both east and west ranges originally even had open cloistered walkways on the north facade. This style visually captured the unique mix of public function and private monies, as well as the English origin, represented by James Smithson's bequest. It was a distinction expressed as well in the choice of building material. The red sandstone, quarried in Seneca, Maryland, mostly likely by enslaved African American laborers, stood in striking contrast to the pale Aquia Creek sandstone used for the capital's earlier public buildings.

The architect was James Renwick Jr. (1818–95), a talented and well-connected twenty-eight-year-old New Yorker, who won the 1846 competition held by the building committee of the newly chartered Smithsonian. Renwick was the son of an amateur architect and already much admired for his Gothic Revival Grace Church in New York City, which he had designed in 1843. The style of the Smithsonian building was intended from the beginning as a model for the nation. Even before it was completed, the design was discussed in an 1849 book, *Hints on Public Architecture*, in which Robert Dale Owen (1801–77), a regent who was the building committee chairman, made the case for a new, picturesque national style of architecture for America.

The building had to house many activities. When Congress passed the 1846 act establishing the Smithsonian Institution, it called for the creation of a museum, laboratories, a library, lecture halls, a gallery of art, and more. Believing that the institution's success depended on a building that could "make conspicuous the work of the organization," Owen advocated a large, showy structure. The accommodation of these multifaceted functions is still readable on the Castle's exterior.

The Romanesque-style Castle (above and left) was first presented to the public in the 1849 book Hints on Public Architecture. Robert Dale Owen, a congressman and regent of the Smithsonian, was the author. The book (frontispiece, right) argued that a medieval revival style, as exemplified by the Smithsonian building, should be the basis for a new national architecture.

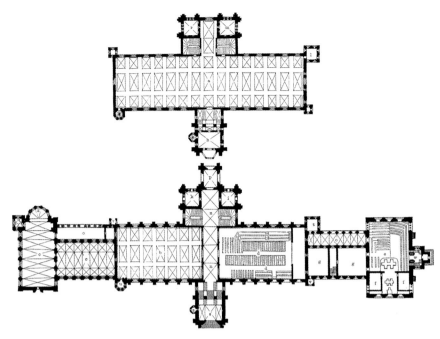

James Renwick's floor plan of the Smithsonian's first building (left), published in Hints on Public Architecture, shows the earliest configuration of the Castle.

Three of the Castle's nine towers catch the early morning light (opposite).

Andrew J. Russell photographed the Castle (below) right before the Civil War, when the grounds around the institution were planted in a romantic style laid out by Andrew Jackson Downing.

In 1849 the stout eastern end of the building, with its heavy crenellation and contrastingly delicate chimney-pot piers, became the first part to be completed. For nearly a year, all of the work of the Smithsonian was carried out within its walls. Once the entire building was finished in 1855, this original section provided office and laboratory space and the important International Exchange Service, which disseminated scientific publications around the world. For twenty-three years it also contained living quarters for the Smithsonian's first secretary, Joseph Henry, and his family. In the Smithsonian's first decades, others lived in the building as well, including a number of young naturalists who had bedrooms high up in the towers. The east wing of the building underwent a major reconstruction in 1883–84, after Joseph Henry's death. New floors of office space were inserted in fireproof materials by Adolf Cluss and Paul Schulze, the architects of the Smithsonian's second building, the Arts and Industries Building.

The Castle's west wing resembles a chapel. Beautifully lighted, with skylights and a rose window as well as clerestory windows, the west wing was intended originally as a gallery of art. It later served as exhibition space, but when the building first opened this area contained the Smithsonian's library.

The Castle's massive south tower (opposite), with its crenellated cornice, rises out of the Enid A. Haupt Garden. Visible in a niche is a medieval sculpture of St. Dunstan, patron saint of blacksmiths, which was donated in 1980 by Westminster Abbey. Nineteenth-century garden furniture, reflective of the building's Victorian origins, is scattered throughout the grounds. The garden also features a Carrara-marble urn (below), designed by Calvert Vaux and erected on the Smithsonian grounds in 1856 to honor the landscape designer Andrew Jackson Downing.

Visitors view the natural history collections in the two-hundred-foot-long Great Hall, two years after the end of the Civil War. Balconies encircled the space, which today is still dominated by two rows of immense arched piers.

The chapel-like west wing (opposite), with its rose window and vaulted ceiling, originally housed the institution's library and today features exhibition objects from many Smithsonian museums.

The central block, with its giant two-story rounded windows, accommodated the museum galleries and other public functions. By placing the staircases in the towers, the main floors could be left open. The grand, central space on the ground floor, now called the Great Hall, was originally some two hundred feet long; it is dominated by two rows of immense arched piers, each consisting of clusters of slender columns culminating in delicate, ornate capitals. The upper story, in its first iteration, housed a lecture hall that could accommodate 1,500 persons, an art gallery, and an apparatus room where scientific experiments were demonstrated. In 1865 the upper portion of the building was destroyed in a fire. When it was rebuilt, using fireproof materials, the space was put to new use. It became a museum gallery, housing many of the items that would form the core of the Natural History Museum collections.

The Children's Room (above) opened in 1901 with the theme Knowledge Begins in Wonder. The decorative scheme by Grace Lincoln Temple, the exhibits of live birds and fish, and the cases at child's-eye level were all designed to engage young visitors.

The Smithsonian's National Zoo had its start behind the Castle in the late 1880s, with American bison—then in danger of extinction. This pair was brought to Washington by the institution's taxidermist, William Temple Hornaday.

The Smithsonian quickly became the natural repository for the government's scientific collections. In 1858 all of the items that had been on display at the Patent Office, many of them from the US Exploring Expedition of 1838–42, began to be transferred to the Castle. As the government continued to explore the West, more and more specimens were shipped back to Washington. Soon the burgeoning collections threatened to overwhelm the Smithsonian building. The responsibilities that came with curating these objects drove the first secretary to seek an appropriation from Congress in 1858 for their care; this marked the beginning within the Smithsonian of the US National Museum, which received funding for its own structure (the Arts and Industries Building) in 1879.

Most of the Smithsonian's later museums and many of its research programs had their start in or around the Castle. A Children's Room was created in the South Tower in 1901, with a decorative scheme by the designer Grace Lincoln Temple; its cases were at children's eye level and the objects had labels in English rather than Latin. Other Smithsonian initiatives—such as the Radiation Biology Laboratory, the graphic arts collections, and the ethnology, archeology, and anthropology collections—also had their beginnings in the Castle. Even the National Zoological Park emerged from the South Yard behind the building, where bison threatened with extinction in the West were kept for several years in the late 1880s. The Smithsonian is also one of very few museums in the world to hold the tomb of its founder. James Smithson's remains, housed today in a crypt that features Smithson's original Italian sarcophagus–shaped grave marker, were brought from Italy in the early twentieth century by Alexander Graham Bell.

Queen Elizabeth visits James Smithson's crypt at the Castle's north entrance during the US Bicentennial in 1976. Behind her are Chief Justice Warren Burger, head of the Board of Regents, and Secretary S. Dillon Ripley.

As the Smithsonian expanded and new museum buildings were constructed, the Castle's role changed. In 1970 the building became host to a center for scholars, with the upper hall divided into two floors to accommodate the new Woodrow Wilson International Center for Scholars (now located nearby in the Ronald Reagan Building and International Trade Center). A National Historic Landmark since 1965, the Castle functions as the institution's administrative heart and contains the offices of top Smithsonian officials. It is furnished with Victorian furniture and decorative arts from the Castle Collection, one of the country's few collections of historic furniture to be actively used. Since 1972 a welcome center has been housed in the Great Hall, providing an orientation to the many museums that grew out of this building, the first home of the National Museum. Today, plans are underway for a total rehabilitation of the Castle, to refresh its mechanical equipment, retrofit the building for environmental reasons, and restore its historic areas.

ARTS AND INDUSTRIES BUILDING

The Arts and Industries Building, which opened in 1881, was the first structure specifically designed to house the US National Museum. With its exuberant Victorian polychrome work, the building stands today as one of the great examples of nineteenth-century exposition architecture in the nation. Built quickly and inexpensively of fireproof masonry construction, it was groundbreaking for its time in size, floor plan, and use of technology. Throughout much of its history, the building served as an incubator for the latest in exhibition design. In fact, four future Smithsonian museums—Natural History, American History, American Art, and Air and Space—emerged from collections originally displayed in this building.

Ornament throughout the Arts and Industries Building, such as this medallion detail of an exterior gate, followed the ideals of nineteenth-century reformers who called for designs derived from nature.

The need for a new museum arose directly from the overcrowding of the original Smithsonian building. The space problem in the Castle had become dire by the 1870s, when the Smithsonian began amassing new material to display at the Philadelphia Centennial Exhibition of 1876. Exhibits there focused on the institution's work and featured "a display of the mineral and animal resources, as well as of the ethnology, of the United States." At the conclusion of the fair, all of these objects, together with those of many federal agencies and a number of exhibits presented by foreign governments, made their way by the trainload to the Smithsonian. The overload caused Spencer F. Baird (1823–87), the head of the museum and the man who would become the institution's second secretary, to declare a state of emergency. Appeals were made to Congress, which authorized funding for a new building in 1879.

The architects selected by the building committee for the new museum, Adolf Cluss (1825–1905) and Paul Schulze (1827–97), had come to the United States from Germany in 1848, the year of the European revolutions. Cluss had been active in radical circles and corresponded with Karl Marx for several years, even after the architect had moved to the United States. Notwithstanding his early political ties, he thrived in the American capital, founded the local Republican Party, and was a prominent Washington, DC, citizen. From 1862 to 1876, he designed or oversaw all of the public buildings erected by the District of Columbia government. Cluss's reputation as an outstanding engineer-architect was an important factor in his selection by the Smithsonian. He was later instrumental in renovations at the Castle and the Old Patent Office Building after major fires.

Cluss and Schulze's design for the National Museum, which echoed the pavilion-style buildings popular at the 1876 Philadelphia fair, focused on providing maximum floor space for exhibitions. Some 328 feet square, it was divided into four quadrants, using an equilateral floor plan that took its inspiration from writings on ideal museums by the French theorist J. N. L. Durand. The building's external design was generated by this plan, with each entrance flanked by symmetrical towers and incorporating a tiled, covered vestibule to protect visitors from inclement weather.

The colorful Arts and Industries Building, with its expostion-style layout and abundant natural light, exemplified the latest in museum design at the time of its opening in 1881.

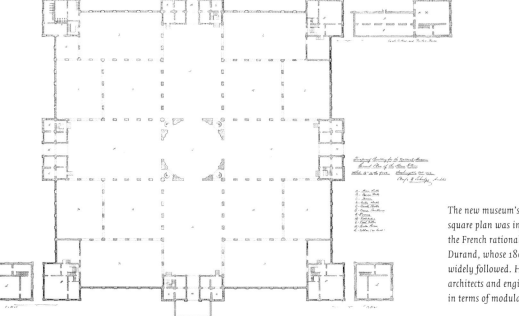

The new museum's equilateral square plan was influenced by the French rationalist J. N. L. Durand, whose 1805 work was widely followed. He taught architects and engineers to think in terms of modular units.

The rapid construction of the new National Museum Building (above) was documented by the Smithsonian photographer Thomas W. Smillie from the roof of the Castle.

The building committee for the National Museum stands in an unfinished doorway of the new building (right). From left to right are General Montgomery C. Meigs; General William Tecumseh Sherman, building committee chairman; Peter Parker, a regent; Spencer F. Baird, Smithsonian secretary; Adolf Cluss, architect; W. J. Rhees, chief clerk; and Daniel Leech, correspondence clerk.

The interior layout was unprecedented in its use of an open-wall interpretation of the Durand plan. Seventeen halls were organized around a central rotunda, with four main double-height halls extending in cardinal directions. Openings in the masonry walls permitted light to pour in from skylights and clerestory windows above and then filter through every public space in the building. Four entrances at ground level, at the cardinal points of the building, reflected Baird's desire to create a welcoming museum for the people, not an elite or rarified institution. Cluss and Schulze, respectful of the Romanesque style of the original Smithsonian building, used rounded arches throughout the interior and the exterior to complement the Castle. The walls were ornamented with stenciled decorative borders and panels, in colors derived from nature—from bright yellow sunlight to deep lavender shadows.

Even before the building officially opened to the public, it hosted President James A. Garfield's inaugural ball in March 1881. While in Congress, Garfield had served as a regent of the Smithsonian. More than five thousand guests attended, many arriving in carriages. The interior was filled with flowers, tropical plants, sculpture, flags, and draped bunting. Gas lighting was temporarily installed inside for the event, which prompted the city's *Evening Star* to report that the ball was "the largest and most brilliantly held . . . the new museum building was conspicuous from a long distance, its lights within giving a good view of its outlines and making it resemble a crystal palace."

The first event held in the new building was President James A. Garfield's inaugural ball on March 4, 1881.

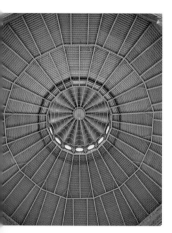

With its polychrome brickwork, slate-covered turrets, and arched windows of Belgian glass, the exterior's whimsical appearance disguises the fact that the building—under thirty-seven separate roof structures—was one of the most technologically innovative of its time. Exposed on the interior, the roof support system was made of wrought-iron trusses; this new technology, developed following the Civil War, was stronger and lighter than cast iron and not prone to rust. At the ridge line, the roof also supported lanterns (long galleried windows) that could ventilate the interior as hot air rose. The enormous operable windows of the main exhibition spaces provided both light and ventilation. Hot water heating, gas and electric lighting, telegraph lines, telephones, sewer connections, and even burglar alarms were all part of this state-of-the-art building when it opened. Bricks, in red and buff, were fabricated with a new hydraulic pressed-brick method. Their use reflected the latest architectural theories: strong horizontal bands of black-colored bricks signaled structural elements, such as towers, buttresses, and pavilions; bricks with smooth, glazed color finishes created a yellow and blue basket-weave pattern to indicate the decorative and non-load-bearing curtain walls. Corbelling (stepping) of bricks provided a pleasing texture at the cornice line, while terra-cotta medallions set between arched windows in the ranges featured plant-inspired designs.

The simple appearance of the roof above the interior rotunda hides a sophisticated design (above). Rigid supports in alternating straight and angled positions produce a hypnotic pattern.

A cast-zinc sculptural group, Columbia Protecting Science and Industry, by Caspar Buberl (right), rises over the Mall entrance. Representing the nation, Columbia wears a headdress of five-pointed stars. The figure Science is reading a book with an owl, representing knowledge, while Industry holds the tools of the nineteenth century's new industries.

Visitors flocked to the new museum, which was free and open to all, at the turn of century (opposite). The formal limestone-framed entrance is one of four into the building.

The light-filled south hall is seen as it appeared in 1885, shortly after the installation of taxidermist Joseph Palmer's half-cast and skeleton of a humpback whale.

Within a few years, however, the building was overflowing with collections, a problem that persisted even after balconies were inserted in the four corner courts in 1897–1902 by local architects Hornblower and Marshall. These mezzanine spaces, with Beaux Arts–detailed iron railings as well as stairs connecting to the rotunda, increased space for a while, but as the collections grew even larger, staff continued to complain of the lack of storage and work space. After nearly twenty years of appeals for a new building, Congress appropriated $3.5 million in 1903. When the new National Museum of Natural History was completed across the Mall in 1911, it was dedicated to the collections of natural and human history. The Smithsonian's nascent gallery of art was also transferred to the new museum. Cluss and Schulze's innovative structure retained the collections emphasizing the industrial arts, technology, and American history, and it was renamed the Arts and Industries Building.

Its collections, which became the core of the future Museum of History and Technology (today the National Museum of American History), also eventually outgrew the building. When the Smithsonian embarked on an exhibition modernization program in the 1950s and 1960s, many ideas were tested first at the Arts and Industries Building. The Museum of History and Technology, completed in 1964, became the showpiece of the Smithsonian's newest presentation ideas. Arts and Industries was then transformed into a site for temporary exhibitions, but it continued to be dominated by growing air and space collections. Planes such as the Wright Brothers' 1903 Flyer and Lindbergh's Spirit of St. Louis hung overhead in the galleries, and the group of rockets forming Rocket Row rose high over the building's west side. The opening of the National Air and Space Museum in 1976 freed up the building once more.

Now a National Historic Landmark, Arts and Industries underwent an extensive rehabilitation in the 1970s under the direction of the noted local architect Hugh Newell Jacobsen (1929–2021). The four two-story internal courts were filled in to provide additional office and work space, and the building systems and roof were upgraded. The building reopened in time for the US Bicentennial celebrations in 1976, with a popular exhibition recreating the 1876 Philadelphia Centennial Exhibition. The exhibition and the building were so well suited that visitors could feel they were stepping back in time.

During the 1990s and early 2000s, the Arts and Industries building housed a variety of temporary art, history, and horticulture exhibitions, as well as the popular Discovery Theatre and the Experimental Gallery. In 2004, however, the building was closed to the public because of structural deterioration. The initial rehabilitation of the building in 2012–14 involved the replacement of the roof, the repointing of the brick, and reopening of the four internal courts. Beginning in 2015 the building began reopening for special events, and in 2021, as part of the Smithsonian's 175th anniversary, it will host an exposition titled FUTURES. In 2022, the building will close once more for a major revitalization of the interior, with restored finishes and new mechanical systems.

After an extensive renovation, the Smithsonian opened an exhibition, 1876, recreating the Centennial Exposition in Philadelphia. The Arts and Industries Building had originally been erected to house many of the objects from that world's fair.

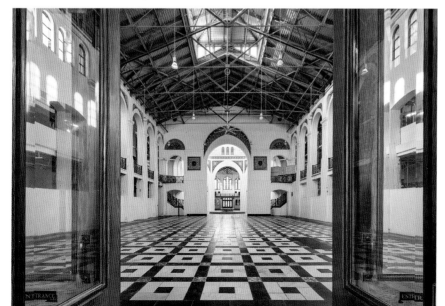

The architecture of the museum reveals itself most fully when emptied of all collections.

National Zoo and Conservation Biology Institute

At the time of its founding in 1889, the National Zoological Park was unlike any other zoo in the world. Most nineteenth-century zoos, such as ones in Philadelphia and Cincinnati, were small urban menageries designed primarily for the entertainment of visitors. The National Zoo was the first zoo planned as a breeding park and a wildlife refuge for the preservation of North American species. It encompassed approximately 170 acres in Rock Creek Park, on what was then the outskirts of Washington, DC.

William Ralph Emerson's Buffalo House of 1891 evoked the rustic log cabins of the American frontier. It was demolished in the 1930s.

The zoo was the inspiration of the Smithsonian's taxidermist, William Temple Hornaday (1854–1937). On a collecting trip to Montana in the late 1880s, he was shocked at the decimation of the American bison, which he called "the most striking and conspicuous species on this continent." Hornaday enlisted

the Smithsonian to help secure the animal's preservation and published *The Extermination of the American Bison*. While Congress debated a proposal to establish a zoological park, the seeds of the National Zoo began with a group of live bison Hornaday maintained behind the Castle. Believing that the zoo would principally benefit local residents—rather than serve as a national endeavor—Congress initially created it in conjunction with the District of Columbia and specified that half of its budget come from the city.

The physical plan for the zoo was conceived by the famed landscape architect Frederick Law Olmsted (1822–1903), the designer of Central Park in New York City. It featured a long, broad, winding path (today called Olmsted Walk), with the main buildings clustered together at the center of the property. Olmsted's fellow Massachusetts architect William Ralph Emerson designed a number of the early animal houses, such as the Buffalo Barn and the first Lion House (known variously at first as the Carnivora House). These picturesque buildings, made of rustic, local stone or wood, were meant to evoke ideas of the American wilderness.

Children in their Easter best stand in front of the old Carnivora or Lion and Tiger House in 1936. The National Zoo began hosting Easter Monday events for African American families in the 1890s, a time when legalized racial discrimination meant they were excluded from the White House Easter Egg Roll. Easter Monday continues today and is open to all.

The National Zoo experienced a heyday in the first half of the twentieth century under William Mann (1886–1960), a gregarious and enterprising leader who served as director for more than twenty-five years. He (and often his wife, Lucile Quarry Mann) traveled around the world on expeditions, such as the Smithsonian-Chrysler Expedition to East Africa in 1926, the National Geographic-Smithsonian Expedition to the Dutch East Indies in 1937, and the Firestone-Smithsonian Expedition to Liberia in 1940, bringing thousands of animals to the zoo. Many of the major animal houses were built during these years, including the Reptile House, the Bird House, the Elephant House, and the Small Mammal House. These buildings, designed by the municipal architect of Washington (first Albert Harris, and then Edward Clarke), were full of whimsy and architectural decoration, underscoring the emphasis on popular entertainment that flourished in these years. The structures incorporated animal imagery and sculpture inside and out, often in new, unusual materials, such as aluminum and colored concrete. Many of the pieces were created during the Great Depression by artists with the federal Works Progress Administration.

The fantastical Reptile House by Albert Harris was completed in 1931. Designed in a Byzanto-Romanesque style, it features innovative polychrome cast-concrete decorative pilasters designed by John Joseph Earley and lots of reptilian imagery. Artist Charles Robert Knight created the stegosaurus mosaic tympanum above the entrance.

The 1928 Bird House (left), designed by Albert Harris, featured an ornate cast-concrete entrance by artist Stephen Haweis. This entrance is now installed in the interior of the building.

The Lion and Tiger House by Faulkner, Fryer and Vanderpool (opposite) was one of several concrete earthwork structures built at the zoo in the 1970s.

The Great Flight Cage (bottom), enabling visitors to enter the birds' space, was designed in a soaring, modernist style by Richard Dimon of Daniel, Mann, Johnson and Mendenhall, in 1963.

By the late 1950s the zoo's physical plant was deteriorating. A fatal accident at the Lion House in 1958 forced the closure of six buildings and led to the creation of the Friends of the National Zoo. FONZ's first achievement was to persuade Congress to fund the zoo's entire budget, which eliminated the prior reliance on District of Columbia government appropriations and enabled the Smithsonian to embark on a period of renovation and renewal in Rock Creek. The zoo undertook a master plan in 1961 and then, from 1972 to 1990, an extensive new plan created by Faulkner, Fryer and Vanderpool. The buildings of the latter period—among them the Lion and Tiger House, the Great Ape House, and the administration building at the Connecticut Avenue entrance—were all concrete earthworks set into the land. They embodied the period's growing environmental awareness and emphasis on conservation. The popular giant pandas that are such a symbol of the zoo today first arrived from China in 1972, following President Richard M. Nixon's historic visit; their addition to the zoo reflected the organization's commitment to the study and preservation of endangered species and their habitats.

In the 1970s the National Zoo also acquired a large property in the Shenandoah Valley near Front Royal, Virginia, which serves today as the headquarters for the Smithsonian Conservation Biology Institute. This 3,200-acre preserve, an army facility erected in 1912–16 to breed and train cavalry horses, is central to the institution's global efforts to save wildlife species from extinction and prepare future generations of conservationists. At SCBI, research scientists study and propagate rare species (including some like the black-footed ferret, the most endangered mammal in the United States) and reintroduce them in the wild. In 2008, the Smithsonian partnered with George Mason University to establish the Smithsonian-Mason School of Conservation, building new dorms, a classroom building, and a cafeteria.

The 1992 Amazonia building by Cooper-Lecky Architects presents the ecosystem of a rain forest together with the animals that live in it.

The zoo introduced the idea of a BioPark in the late 1980s, emphasizing exhibits that displayed entire ecosystems to visitors. These installations show plants and animals living together in their native environments, rather than relegating plants to a decorative or supporting role. Amazonia (1992)—at fifteen thousand square feet the largest and most complex exhibit at the zoo—reflects this approach. It is a rainforest habitat featuring more than 350 plant species and dozens of species of mammals, birds, reptiles, amphibians, and insects native to the Amazon basin.

The National Zoo's most recent master plan called for the renovation of the Bird House as a Migratory Bird Center and for new visitor amenities. Animal habitats are being upgraded to reflect contemporary advances in knowledge of animal health and well-being. The plan also calls for the continued protection of the zoo's historic properties and the Rock Creek ecosystem. The Asia Trail, which debuted in 2006, leads visitors through a series of habitats and encounters with seven species, such as sloth bears, red pandas, and Asian small-clawed otters. It includes the David M. Rubenstein Family Giant Panda Habitat, which mimics China's rocky, lush landscape and features grottoes and streams, bamboo stands and weeping willows, as well as a state-of-the-art research facility. Elephant Trails, an essential component of the zoo's Asian elephant conservation program, is a reconfiguration of the old Elephant House and surrounding areas intended to enable the animals to live as a herd and range more freely over a larger area. In keeping with the aims of the zoo, these new exhibits are closely entwined with the institution's research and conservation efforts.

The American Trails exhibit, which opened in 2012, showcases animals native to the United States and Canada, including wolves, beavers, otters, seals, pelicans, and eagles. Immersing visitors in a North American habitat, it was built using sustainable practices and reutilized elements of a 1970s exhibit, Beaver Valley.

NATIONAL MUSEUM OF NATURAL HISTORY

The 2020 restoration of the south entrance by Quinn Evans Architects included two new accessibility switchback walkways.

The National Museum of Natural History, which opened to the public in 1910 (a year before its completion), was the first building constructed on the Mall to reflect the ideals of the 1901 McMillan Commission. Intended to revive the eighteenth-century proposals of Pierre Charles L'Enfant for the federal city of Washington, the McMillan Plan reinstated the goal of monumental classicism and brought with it a sober Roman style. It transformed the Mall from a romantic, forested landscape with curving carriageways to the sweeping, open, formal greensward so familiar today, stretching from the Capitol to the Washington Monument. In its siting and its style, the Natural History Museum served as a prototype for a Beaux-Arts Washington.

The Washington, DC, firm Hornblower and Marshall was selected to design the museum. At the time, it served as house architect for the Smithsonian, designing everything from Smithson's crypt and the Children's Room in the Castle to buildings at the zoo. To prepare for this monumental new building—intended also to embody the latest ideas for museum display, research laboratories, and public spaces—the architects made a tour of European museums. They studied all aspects of design, especially space allotment, exhibition cases, and lighting, noting exemplary placements of windows and skylights.

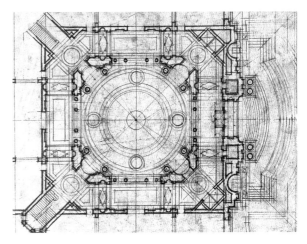

Hornblower and Marshall's original drawing shows the formal floor plan of the three-story domed rotunda, from which all parts of the building radiate.

At the same time the head curators, notably William Henry Holmes, curator of prehistoric archeology, searched for model buildings. They canvassed museums around the world, asking for photographs, floor plans, guidebooks, and drawings. Holmes greatly influenced the successful plan for the Natural History Museum, particularly by calling for a large lecture hall. The building, as one Smithsonian official noted, marked "the beginning of a new year in the history of the National Museum, through the unrivaled conditions presented for the arrangement, care and safety of the collections." Richard Rathbun, a geologist who came to the institution in 1881, was appointed an assistant secretary in 1901; he oversaw the design and construction of the new building from 1901 until its completion.

In 1905 the Smithsonian, unhappy with the ornate design of the planned dome, halted construction. Hornblower and Marshall experimented with ever-bolder articulations of the central pavilion and increased the dome's height, but Secretary Samuel P. Langley continued to withhold his approval. The impasse continued for a year, until it was broken by the design intervention of Daniel Burnham (1846–1912) and Charles Follen McKim (1847–1909) of McKim, Mead & White. McKim and Burnham were key members of the McMillan Commission, and Burnham was also the architect of one of its showpieces, Union Station, and the adjacent main post office (today the Smithsonian's National Postal Museum). McKim and Burnham substituted a sober, low Roman dome, tiled and placed on an attic story with semicircular windows based on those at the Baths of Diocletian. They also designed the massive columned portico facing the Mall, making the revised design a model for the classical buildings the McMillan Commission envisioned for Washington's monumental core.

The fish-scale-tile dome of the Natural History Museum stands out from other local landmarks, including the FBI Building in the foreground and Reagan National Airport and the Masonic Temple in Alexandria, Virginia, in the distance at right.

The Smithsonian was thrilled with the dignified tone set by the new concept and immediately restarted construction. When the museum was completed in 1911, it was one of the largest public buildings in Washington (at more than one million square feet), second only to the Capitol. Hailed by the *Washington Post* as "the most remarkable structure of its kind in the world," it proved immensely popular and became the first Smithsonian museum to offer Sunday hours to accommodate the large number of visitors.

As befits the first Smithsonian museum of the twentieth century, this building is supported on a steel frame and includes two-story-high steel windows with decorative rosettes on the mullions. In contrast to the classical severity of the exterior, faced in granite, the interior central pavilion contains a dramatic, three-story octagonal domed rotunda. The subtle dome was constructed in the thin-shell technique devised by the Catalan architect Rafael Guastavino (1842–1908). On the level beneath the rotunda is the auditorium, an elegant circular room also sporting a Guastavino-tile dome. The great space of the rotunda has been dominated since 1959 by an enormous African bush elephant, which at the time of its unveiling was the largest land mammal on display in a museum. From this spot the building expands in three directions—south, west, and east—with grand, three-story-high halls lighted by skylights. This T-shaped plan originally incorporated two courtyards, providing light and air to the offices and laboratories encircling them; these have now been enclosed. For a quarter century the building's coal furnaces supplied heat and hot water to the other Smithsonian buildings, using steam tunnels under the Mall.

An enormous, thirteen-foot-tall African elephant has been the centerpiece of the rotunda since 1959.

An aerial view of the museum in the early 1960s, before construction of the west wing, shows the new east wing at the right. The two original courtyards were filled in during the 1990s for an IMAX theater (since removed) and visitor amenities on the west side and offices on the east.

The increasing breadth of the collections documenting the study of humans, plants, animals, and prehistory meant that yet again it was not long before additional space was required. In 1930 Congress authorized the construction of wings, but these were not funded until 1960. Designed by Mills, Petticord and Mills, the six-story wings that were erected in the early 1960s were dedicated entirely to collections and staff laboratories. Their form, a modest modern interpretation of the original building, was shaped by two review standards: one, that additions to historic buildings avoid exactly copying the original design, and two, that the wings be set back from the main facade. With the expansion provided by this new space, the museum grew to eventually occupy just under two million square feet.

The Hall of Extinct Monsters (above), now known as the Hall of Fossils—Deep Time, included the mural painting Diana of the Tides (1908), by John Eliot, in the background.

The museum was closed to the public from 1917 to 1919 for wartime activities. Hundreds of desks filled the exhibition space, where employees of the Bureau of War Risk Insurance worked (left).

The Sant Ocean Hall opened in 2008. A scale model of a forty-five-foot-long North Atlantic right whale is suspended from the ceiling of the restored, skylit space.

As the Smithsonian embarked on an institution-wide campaign of exhibition modernization in the 1950s and 1960s, many of the Natural History Museum's halls were altered through renovations. Air conditioning and fluorescent lighting installed when the wings were constructed eliminated the need for natural light and open windows. Neoclassical details and skylights were hidden behind curving, modernistic display cases and dioramas.

The Smithsonian's expansion into new buildings in the 1960s also had a significant impact on the Natural History Museum and its contents. With the creation of the American Art Museum and the Portrait Gallery in the Old Patent Office Building, the gallery of art (which had come to the Smithsonian in 1906) finally moved out. And with the 1964 opening of the Museum of History and Technology (now the National Museum of American History), collections including domestic life, musical instruments, and cultural history—which had all fallen under the flexible rubric of the anthropology department—left the building as well.

In the last two decades the museum has restored its spectacular three-story grand halls: the Kenneth E. Behring Family Hall of Mammals (2003), the Sant Ocean Hall (2008), and the David H. Koch Hall of Fossils—Deep Time (2019). In the east internal courtyard, the museum built a state-of-the-art facility for the Joseph F. Cullman III Rare Book Library; in the west court, the IMAX theater installed in 1999 has been replaced with food services and upgraded public amenities. Other renovations and additions in the last decades, such as the penthouse additions to the wings for new mechanical equipment and the chiller plant located at the southeast corner of the property, have taken their inspiration from the original Hornblower and Marshall design. The 1960s windows in the west and east wings were replaced with replicas of the originals in the main building, giving a more uniform look to the entire structure. An important change to the south entrance of the building was the addition of symmetrical ramps at either side of the monumental steps, making both historic entrances accessible. Today the Natural History Museum is one of the most popular museums in the world, receiving some 4.5 million visitors a year.

The Hall of Fossils—Deep Time explores the evolution of plant and animal life over billions of years.

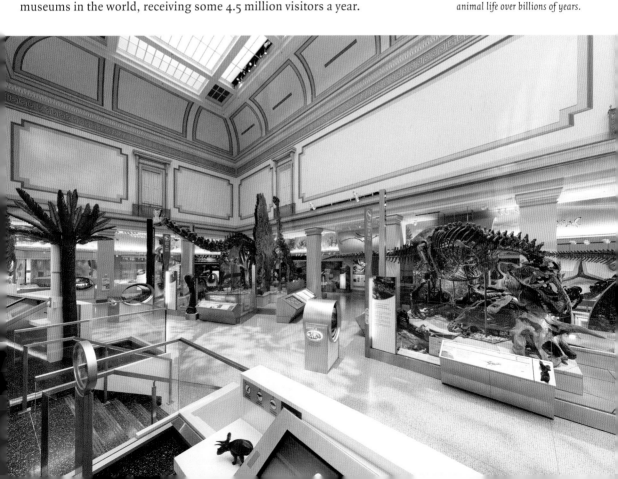

FREER GALLERY OF ART

The Freer Gallery of Art, the first Smithsonian museum devoted exclusively to the fine arts, was a gift to the nation from the Detroit industrialist Charles Lang Freer. Over a lifetime he amassed the country's most outstanding private collection of Asian art. Freer's initial donation of 2,250 objects offered in 1904 was more than quadrupled by additional donations he made during the next decade. His gift also included funds for a building to house all of his collections and an endowment to support research and future acquisitions.

The son of an innkeeper, Freer (1854–1919) was born in Kingston, New York, and left school at age fourteen to work in a cement factory. His relentless drive and attention to detail brought him great success. He earned his fortune in the manufacture of railroad cars and retired at age forty-five to dedicate himself to his art collecting.

The unparalleled Asian art collections of the Detroit industrialist Charles Lang Freer were donated to the nation to create the Freer Gallery of Art. Freer died before seeing his gift enjoyed by visitors.

Freer made many lengthy trips to China and Japan over the course of his life, visiting temples, porcelain factories, collectors, and viceroys of far-flung provinces in search of the finest works of art. His first Asian art purchase, in 1887, was a painted Japanese fan. He amassed works dating from Neolithic times to the twentieth century, including one of the world's best collections of ancient metalwork and weaponry. The collection includes Chinese bronzes, jades, ceramics, paintings, lacquerware, and textiles; early Buddhist sculpture; Japanese screens, Ukiyo-e paintings, and tea ceremony objects; illuminated manuscripts from the Islamic world; ancient Egyptian amulets and statuary; elaborately decorated ancient Near Eastern silver vessels; temple sculpture from Cambodia, Vietnam, and Thailand; and Mughal paintings.

Charles A. Platt's floor plan reflects Freer's early vision, sketched on Plaza Hotel stationery in 1913 (right), for his museum— with galleries arranged around a central courtyard.

Freer's interest in Asian art developed as an outgrowth of his support for contemporary American artists, particularly James McNeill Whistler (1834–1903), who was profoundly influenced by Japanese artistic traditions. Freer's collection of Whistler's works is one of the largest in the world and includes the artist's only surviving example of interior decoration, the famous *Harmony in Blue and Gold: The Peacock Room*, once a private

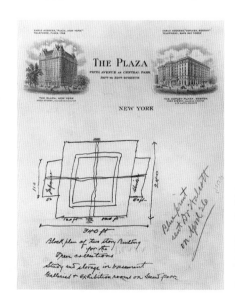

dining room in London. Freer also collected the works of Thomas Wilmer Dewing, Abbott Handerson Thayer, Dwight William Tryon, and other American artists, to whom Freer was both patron and friend. Under the terms of Freer's bequest, the museum's collection of American art is not to be augmented or changed.

It was through these artists that he met the artist and landscape architect Charles A. Platt (1861–1933), whom he later commissioned to design the museum building. The two men shared a philosophy of art for art's sake—a devotion to the idea of beauty. Just as Whistler had encouraged Freer's interest in Asia, so Platt advised him on principles of classical garden design and devised a tour of Italian Renaissance gardens for him.

When Freer approached Platt to design his museum, he came to the architect with some definite design ideas. In an early sketch that he drew for Platt on the stationery of his New York hotel, a number of the final building's key features are evident. A peaceful central courtyard, the placement of study and storage areas in the basement, and the disposition of exhibition spaces on the main floor—with Chinese galleries on one side, Japanese on the other, and American art in the interlinking spaces—were all retained by Platt in the ultimate Renaissance-inspired design.

In 2017, after an eighteen-month renovation, the Freer reopened with a two-day IlluminAsia festival. The award-winning designers, 59 Productions, projected a twelve-minute history of the museum on the north facade as part of the celebrations.

65

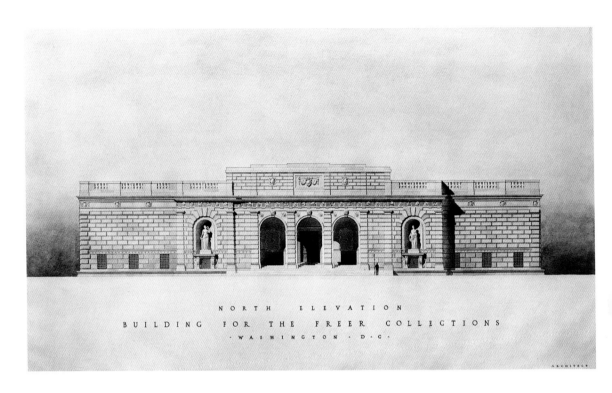

NORTH ELEVATION
BUILDING FOR THE FREER COLLECTIONS
· WASHINGTON · D · C ·

ARCHITECT

The Freer Gallery's palazzo form, round-arch doorways, sculpture niches, parapet walls, and rusticated stonework all evoke a sixteenth-century Italian Renaissance style.

The regents of the Smithsonian deliberated for two years before accepting Freer's gift in 1906. President Theodore Roosevelt, a keen advocate for the collection's acquisition, was instrumental in securing the gift. Together with a bequest of mostly European art from President James Buchanan's niece Harriet Lane Johnston, which the Smithsonian also accepted in 1906, the Freer gift was seen as the beginning of a national collection of art in Washington.

Many cities and organizations had vied for Freer's extraordinary collection, but Washington was a natural home for it. At the turn of the century—a time that elevated the idea of public citizenship—the capital was seen as a second home for Americans, and there was a great desire to beautify it as a symbol of the republic. Freer was a close friend of a fellow Michigan Republican, Senator James McMillan, who led the Senate commission dedicated to returning Washington to the classical ideals of the eighteenth-century L'Enfant Plan. Charles Platt's elegant, restrained Italianate palazzo design for the Freer fit well within the new vision for buildings that would line the Mall.

Construction of the Freer finally began in 1917, but it was almost immediately delayed because of the nation's entry into World War I. Inspired by the works of the Italian Mannerist architect Michele Sanmicheli (1484–1559), the building was faced with Stony Creek granite from Connecticut, selected together by Freer and Platt, who each had a summer home in the western part of the state. The building consists of one principal floor, arranged around a central court, over a raised basement containing the study and storage areas. The windowless facade is enlivened with a balustraded parapet, recessed niches, and decorative friezes. The galleries are lighted by skylights of Luxfer glass, a prismatic material specially designed to provide an even display of natural light.

The construction of the new gallery, seen here in the winter of 1918, was delayed by World War I.

The Freer's north entrance is a portico with three rounded arched openings. The windowless facade is enlivened by arched niches, decorative friezes, and a balustraded parapet at the roofline.

The courtyard, faced with a light pink Tennessee marble, was another essential element of the design from the beginning. Freer saw it as a reminder of the dynamic interaction of art and nature so integral to Asian art. The building opens onto this serene space, with its arcaded cloister and central fountain. And as part of the Smithsonian's ongoing effort to increase access to its historic spaces, this central space is now accessible to all visitors.

Because Freer's bequest included funds for study and research, the building was designed with space for a library and laboratories below ground. Today a large and steadily growing study collection is used by scholars, for laboratory analysis, and for testing conservation methods. The high basement spaces are illuminated by windows delicately inserted beneath the wave-patterned belt-course (midlevel frieze) on the exterior.

A classical wave-motif belt course wraps around the building, ornamenting the austere rusticated facade.

Freer, who died four years before the museum opened in 1923, wished "to unite modern work with masterpieces of certain periods of high civilization, harmonious in spiritual and physical suggestion, having the power to broaden aesthetic culture and the grace to elevate the human mind." His gallery has long fulfilled that goal through its wide-ranging exhibition program, scholarly publications, and research. Over the years the building has not been substantially altered. In conjunction with the creation of the Quadrangle in the late 1980s, basement storage and study capacities were enlarged and an underground connection to the Arthur M. Sackler Gallery was constructed; today the two museums together are called the National Museum of Asian Art.

The arches from the north entrance are echoed in the interior courtyard arcade. This space, visible as visitors move through the galleries, was inspired by the Renaissance buildings Freer loved in Italy.

The building's serene, skylit gallery spaces (right), seen here in the early years of the museum, remain much the same today.

James McNeill Whistler's Harmony in Blue and Gold: The Peacock Room (1876–77) (below and opposite), designed for a London mansion and later purchased by Freer, is an iconic element of the museum.

NATIONAL MUSEUM OF AMERICAN HISTORY

KENNETH E. BEHRING CENTER

The National Museum of American History opened in 1964—the culmination of years of planning and study of the most modern methods of exhibition design. It was the first Smithsonian museum to be built on the Mall since the 1920s, and in its stark modernity it was unlike any previous Smithsonian museum. One of the last major works designed by the venerable architecture firm McKim, Mead & White, the building was "classical in definition, and the detail is modern," explained the principal architect, Walker O. Cain (1915–93). "There's that peripheral parade around a very simple rectangular form that is so disarmingly simple that I think it sits well with neo-classical buildings all around it."

The building was not only stylistically modern; it also reflected a new approach to museum presentation. In the words of Secretary Leonard Carmichael (1898–1973), the museum was designed to be "a great exhibition machine." Under its first director, Frank Taylor, who led the Smithsonian-wide exhibition modernization program at midcentury, the new museum focused on presenting an educational message using the objects as examples of their type. "If the National Museum is to accomplish its mission as defined in the broadest sense," Taylor wrote, "it must be viewed as more than a mere Trophy House— it must be accepted as a vital instrument of national education."

The stripped-down classicism and massing of the National Museum of American History create a colonnade effect reminiscent of the Lincoln Memorial. Cutout openings on the roof cast a "shadow cornice" on the facades, as depicted in this original rendering.

The Washington Monument
rises in the distance behind
the museum's Constitution
Avenue entrance. The fountains
in the forecourt were seen by
the architect as integral to the
design of the building.

Although a museum of engineering and technology had been proposed as
early as 1923, no museums had been built on the Mall since the opening of the
Freer that same year. The overcrowded conditions at the Arts and Industries
Building—where hundreds of objects were still displayed in a nineteenth-
century style, clustered together with little written explanation—helped make
the case for a modern new museum. The Smithsonian was aided as well, Taylor
later said, by "the somewhat exuberant time of national pride after World
War II," when "the need to describe a national museum of the history of the
United States became urgent." President Dwight D. Eisenhower signed the bill
on June 28, 1955, and groundbreaking for what was originally known as the
National Museum of History and Technology took place three years later.

The restrained five-story rectangular building rests on a broad terraced base,
much like a classical Greek temple. This platform, which provides an on-grade
entrance on the Mall, wraps around the building and steps down on the north
facade to the lower grade of Constitution Avenue. The sleek Tennessee marble
surfaces of alternating projecting and recessed bays evoke a kind of abstract
classical colonnade. Cutouts ringing the roof level cast a geometrical silhouette
on the facade that functions as a modernist "shadow cornice."

A detail of the building's "shadow cornice" shows the original windows (now blocked on the interior), which were tucked into the sides of the projecting bays.

In the museum's early years, night lighting helped emphasize the vertical windows and the walls. The underground passage was designed to hide the service entrance and museum parking.

The architect had visited several large museums in Europe and believed strongly that a museum without windows could be disorienting to visitors. He thus inserted partially hidden windows into the sides of the projecting stone-clad bays, allowing some daylight to enter the museum. With lights placed inside the recesses to shine out at night—echoing the lighted, colonnaded Lincoln Memorial to the west—the museum created a striking presence on the Mall.

Entrances for parking and the loading dock were cleverly hidden by green landscaping and by the elevation change between the Mall side and Constitution Avenue. A fountain was designed for the Constitution Avenue entrance, and two sculptures were specially commissioned for the museum: the *Gwenfritz*, by Alexander Calder (1898–1976), placed at the west end, and *Infinity*, by José de Rivera (1904–85), located on the south terrace.

Yugoslav dancers in the 1973 Smithsonian Folklife Festival assemble around José de Rivera's Infinity (1968). At right, at the far end of the terrace, is a cedar shade structure designed by architect Victor Lundy.

More than fifty-four thousand visitors entered the museum's gleaming stainless-steel and glass doors the first Sunday after it opened to the public on January 23, 1964. Two iconic objects in the main entry hall symbolized the museum's dual focus: the Star-Spangled Banner (history) and a Foucault pendulum (technology), which hung through an oculus to the floor below, connecting the first and second levels. The first floor was devoted to technology and science themes, such as transportation and medicine; the second floor focused on American history, with the First Ladies' gowns, political ephemera, and period domestic settings; and the third floor presented a wide range of displays—stamps and coins, printing and photography, ceramics and glass, music, and military history. Many of the collections had their own dedicated space for the first time. The musical instruments, for example, which had been tucked away on the third floor of the Natural History Museum, flourished in a new temperature-controlled gallery and performance space. As Secretary S. Dillon Ripley said, "You could just see all the instruments smiling for the first time in fifty years."

Few permanent walls interrupted the open flow of space. The plan, considered ideal by contemporary museum standards, was designed to be flexible. As the collections grew, however, the museum's spatial plan changed, and many of the original open expanses were partitioned to form additional exhibit spaces and offices. The narrow, almost lancet-like windows of the facade's projecting bays were bricked up to limit temperature fluctuations, and four of the escalators linking the first and second floors were removed.

This Woolworth lunch counter (left) from Greensboro, North Carolina, was the site of a 1960 sit-in that drew national attention to racial segregation and helped lead to the passage of the Civil Rights Act of 1964. The lunch counter was donated to the museum in 1993.

A gift to the Smithsonian, Julia Child's kitchen (below) was relocated from her home in Cambridge, Massachusetts, in 2001. It is a contextual exhibit, in which an entire room is reconstructed so objects can be seen in place.

In 1980 the museum was renamed the National Museum of American History, signifying a shift in its focus. The change drew attention to the iconic objects of American cultural history, long associated with the Smithsonian, that were housed within: Dorothy's ruby slippers, Abraham Lincoln's top hat, the desk on which Thomas Jefferson crafted the Declaration of Independence, among many others. New storytelling exhibits, such as Field to Factory, which examined the great migration of African Americans from the South to the North in the first half of the twentieth century, explored a variety of American history narratives.

The building was closed in 2006 for a major, two-year renovation, with Skidmore, Owings and Merrill, the architecture firm for the Hirshhorn Museum and Sculpture Garden, hired to transform the museum's central core. A three-story atrium, lighted from a new skylight designed to bring light into the center of the building, features a grand staircase linking the first and second floors. A new exhibit space for the Star-Spangled Banner, signaled by an abstract mirrored polycarbonate representation of the flag on the marble wall facing the atrium, was built using the most modern conservation techniques. Additional renovations in the last decade have involved redesigning the western end of the museum interior, with each floor focused on a central theme; enlarging the window on the west facade; and infilling the garage to provide additional support space.

The Star-Spangled Banner, together with a Foucault pendulum that spanned two stories, was the centerpiece of the museum for several decades. This view is from 1993, five years before the pendulum was removed.

In 2008, the core of the museum was reconfigured with a new three-story central atrium (opposite), linked by a grand open stair. An abstract, mirrored polycarbonate representation of the American flag stands at the front of a dedicated exhibition on the Star-Spangled Banner.

SMITHSONIAN AMERICAN ART MUSEUM AND NATIONAL PORTRAIT GALLERY

The Old Patent Office Building, a National Historic Landmark, is considered one of the finest examples of Greek Revival architecture in the United States. It became part of the Smithsonian in 1958, when Congress reassigned this government building for use as the National Collection of Fine Arts (now the Smithsonian American Art Museum) and the National Portrait Gallery. They were the first Smithsonian art museums to be located off the National Mall.

Construction of the Patent Office Building began in 1836, under the presidency of Andrew Jackson, and was finally completed thirty-two years later, under the presidency of Andrew Johnson. Some of the delay was caused by the Civil War, when the building was used as barracks and a hospital for wounded soldiers. Walt Whitman, who visited the soldiers here and at many other temporary hospitals across the city, called the Patent Office "that noblest of Washington buildings."

This daguerreotype by John Plumbe Jr. shows the Patent Office Building around 1846, the year the Smithsonian was founded. The two organizations were closely entwined; the Smithsonian's Board of Regents held their first meetings there, and the exhibits on view at the Patent Office, including James Smithson's effects, eventually made their way to the Castle.

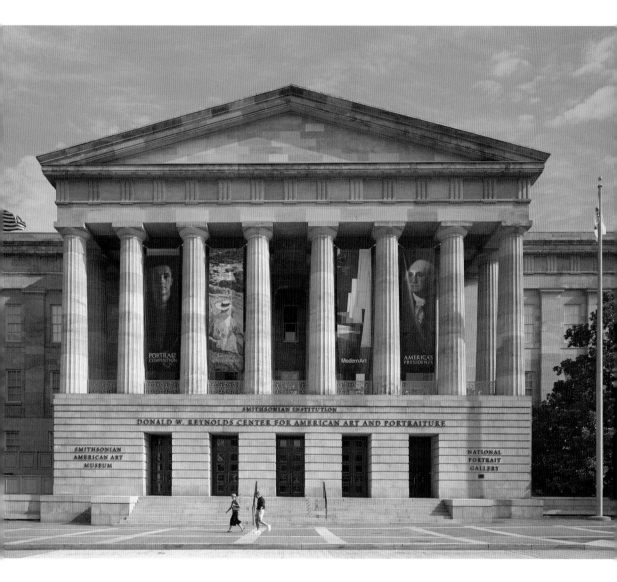

At its completion in 1868, it was the largest building in the United States, covering more than 330,000 square feet. Several of the country's finest nineteenth-century architects supervised its construction, including Robert Mills (1781–1855), the architect of the Washington Monument, and Thomas Ustick Walter (1804–87), the designer of the US Capitol dome. After a disastrous fire in 1877, two wings were rebuilt by Adolf Cluss (1825–1905), the architect of the Smithsonian's Arts and Industries Building.

The entrance to the south wing of the Patent Office Building features a majestic neoclassical portico with eight fluted Doric columns. The original monumental staircase was removed in the 1930s.

The south entrance hall is dominated by Robert Mills's dramatic vaulted ceiling and double staircase. The stair railing was added later by Adolf Cluss as part of his remodeling after the 1877 fire.

This monumental building in the heart of the city's commercial district takes up two blocks and comprises four wings around a courtyard. Mills was responsible for design of the interior and the construction of the original south wing (1836–42), which was built using a local Aquia Creek sandstone (the same light-colored stone that was used for the White House). A spectacular double curved stair leads up to a soaring, groin-vaulted third-floor gallery; its 266-foot space, one of the most impressive in nineteenth-century Washington, showcased the nation's collection of patent models. This "museum of curiosities" gave the building its fame as a "temple of invention."

Cluss's redesign of the Model Hall (opposite and below)—with its colorful encaustic tile floor, elaborate faux-marble finishes, stained glass, and ornate iron railings—provides a striking contrast to the building's original classical austerity.

The next three wings were constructed using white marble for the exterior facades and granite for the interior courtyard facades. The east wing (1849–55), built under Mills's supervision, housed the US Department of the Interior, which included the Indian Office and the Bureau of Agriculture. The west wing (1852–57) and the north wing (1856–68) were supervised by Thomas Walter, who also added the east and west porticoes to the building. Walter changed the structural framing from Mills's brick-vault masonry to a more modern system of iron beams and shallow jack-arch construction. However, these iron beams failed in the 1877 fire, and the top floors of these wings, which housed additional model halls, had to be rebuilt.

Adolf Cluss employed an exuberant "modern Renaissance" style of architecture in the reconstruction of the Model Hall and the Great Hall. These Victorian-era spaces stand in colorful contrast to the more austere classical style of the earlier construction. Skylights added to the roofs after the fire provided natural light for the upper offices and the patent galleries, and stained glass was introduced as a decorative element. Flooring became more colorful as well, with English Minton encaustic tiles laid out in geometric patterns.

Abraham Lincoln's second inaugural ball was held in the Patent Office Building in 1865, just two months before the president's assassination. This space, now used for modern and contemporary art exhibits, survived the 1877 fire.

The building deteriorated greatly during the first half of the twentieth century. The Patent Office moved out in 1932, after which the Civil Service Commission occupied the building until 1963. The building was threatened with demolition for a parking lot and was saved when Congress transferred the building to the Smithsonian in 1958. After extensive renovations, it was opened to the public a decade later. The building provided the first separate home for the Smithsonian's art collections, begun in 1906 and displayed first in the Arts and Industries Building and then for decades amid the Natural History Museum's skeletons and specimens. The American Art Museum, which included the first federal art collection, occupied the north side of the building. The National Portrait Gallery, on the south side, was a new initiative: it focused on telling the story of America through portraits of its people, boosted by a donation of eighteenth-century paintings from Andrew Mellon, the founder of the National Gallery of Art. The building also housed a study center, a library, and, beginning in 1970, the Archives of American Art, one of the most extensive collections of artists' papers in the country. The new Smithsonian museum opened to the public in 1968, after an extensive restoration by the Washington firm Faulkner, Kingsbury and Stenhouse.

The Lincoln Gallery (above), a flexible exhibition space that retains Robert Mills's original groin vaulting, provides a contrasting backdrop for the museum's exhibitions of modern art.

An interior gallery with a maquette of the Statue of Liberty displays a variety of American art (left). The original marble floor was removed during restoration, and each piece was carefully numbered, stored, and cleaned before being reinstalled.

Aging infrastructure and the renewal of the Patent Office Building's neighborhood, spurred by the construction of a new city sports arena, led to another renovation in 2000. This $266 million rehabilitation, completed in 2006 by the Washington, DC, architecture firm Hartman Cox, ushered in a new era for the building as the Donald W. Reynolds Center for American Art and Portraiture. For the first time public spaces for the two museums are integrated; a new auditorium for educational programs is located underneath the central courtyard; and systems throughout the building have been updated with state-of-the-art technology. In 2007 an undulating canopy roof of floating glass and steel, designed by the British architect Norman Foster, Baron Foster of Thames Bank (b. 1935) of Foster and Partners, transformed the courtyard into one of the largest interior spaces in Washington. Landscaped by Kathryn Gustafson (b. 1951) of Gustafson, Guthrie and Nicol in Seattle, the space is beautifully lighted at night.

The Patent Office Building, now one of the jewels of the Smithsonian's building collection, actually has an unusual connection to the institution's early history. Even though it did not become an official Smithsonian building until 1958, it briefly served as the first repository of the Smithsonian collections. In the 1840s, before Congress passed the act establishing the institution, the Patent Office housed James Smithson's mineral collection and his other belongings, which had come to the United States in the 1830s together with the gold coins that represented his bequest. Once the Smithsonian was chartered, it was given space in the Patent Office Building's south wing for gallery and storage use. Specimens from government-sponsored exploratory expeditions destined for the Smithsonian continued to be exhibited here through the 1850s, while the Castle was under construction. It is fitting that this historic public building, restored to its most resplendent condition, is once again a temple to American creativity.

The interior court of the building was enclosed in 2007 to create the Robert and Arlene Kogod Courtyard (opposite). Designed by the British architect Norman Foster, the undulating glass and aluminum canopy is supported by steel columns to prevent having it rest on the historic structure. It is beautifully illuminated in the evening (above).

RENWICK GALLERY OF ART

Built by the banker William Wilson Corcoran to house his personal art collection, this French Second Empire–style landmark was the first public art museum building in Washington. It came into the possession of the Smithsonian in 1965 after a long and eventful history. Now part of the Smithsonian American Art Museum, it is dedicated to contemporary American crafts and decorative arts. The museum's name honors the building's architect, James Renwick Jr., who also designed the Castle, the Smithsonian's first building.

The Renwick Gallery's design, with its tall mansard roofs, was inspired by the French Second Empire style made popular by Napoleon III.

Located across Pennsylvania Avenue from the Eisenhower Executive Office Building (originally the State, War, and Navy Building) in the heart of federal Washington, the Renwick was neglected and then nearly demolished in the mid-twentieth century. At one point it became what the *New York Times* called "a convention hall for pigeons." Thanks to the efforts of First Lady Jacqueline Kennedy to preserve Lafayette Square and the environs of the White House, the building was saved for the nation as part of the revival of Pennsylvania Avenue.

James Renwick (1818–95) began the commission in 1859, a little more than a decade after he had won the commission for the Castle. He and Corcoran (1798–1888) had traveled together in France and took their inspiration for the building, which they imagined as an American Louvre, from the latest architectural style, popularized by the Emperor Napoleon III. Second Empire designs are characterized by steep mansard roofs (often crested with iron detailing), highly decorative surfaces, paired columns, and other sculptural details that project an imposing appearance. The Renwick Gallery is one of the most richly ornamented of the Smithsonian's buildings, its red brick walls embellished with paired brownstone columns and pilasters, elaborately decorated window surrounds, applied stone garlands and cartouches, and ornately carved pediments. This ornament ranges from corncob capitals on the second-floor pilasters to carved medallions with Corcoran's initials, WWC. Above the entrance in bold letters is the inscription, DEDICATED TO ART.

Corcoran, who enslaved people, sided with the Confederacy when the Civil War began. As the building neared completion in 1861, it was seized by the Union Army. Quartermaster General Montgomery C. Meigs (1816–92), the engineer responsible for the design of the Pension Building and the Washington Aqueduct, modified the structure for use as offices, inserting windows in place of blind sculpture niches on the exterior. Corcoran, who spent the war years in France, had difficulty reclaiming his property upon his return, but in 1869, with the help of an influential new board of trustees, he received a charter from Congress to establish a public art gallery. After extensive renovations, his Corcoran Gallery of Art, with an impressive collection of eighteenth- and nineteenth-century art and sculpture from the United States and Europe, opened to the public on January 19, 1874.

A profusion of rich detail on the Renwick Gallery's southwest corner includes corncob capitals on the pilasters and a medallion with the initials WWC for William Wilson Corcoran, the building's original sponsor.

89

The building today is a showcase for contemporary art and craft. Janet Echelman's dramatic fiber and lighting installation 1.8 Renwick in the Grand Salon, using data recorded after the powerful 2011 earthquake and tsunami in Japan, inspired visitors to lie on the carpet underneath to contemplate it.

The museum contained large interconnecting galleries on two floors, surrounding a magnificent grand staircase of mahogany. Ingenious internal light courts (now filled in) as well as skylights in the roof bathed the galleries and the staircase in diffused natural light. The most striking gallery was the double-height Grand Salon on the second floor, which stretched some ninety-five feet across the rear width of the building. Pictures were hung salon style, one above another all across the walls. The first floor had a marble-floored palm court, which is today used as exhibit space. In 1889 an annex was built at the back of the building to house an art school.

Corcoran's collection eventually outgrew its gallery and moved down the street to a new building designed by Ernest Flagg. This new Corcoran Gallery of Art opened in 1897 (a 1928 addition was designed by Charles A. Platt, the architect of the Smithsonian's Freer Gallery of Art); the museum was dissolved in 2014 and the collections distributed to other DC institutions. Corcoran's original building was sold to the federal government in 1901. It became the US Court of Claims, a role ill-suited to the gallery. In its transition to office space, the building suffered from partitioning, the insertion of a steel-beam reinforcement system, and the loss of its exterior iron detail. Perhaps most damaging was the failure to protect the building from water intrusion, which decayed many of the decorative sandstone elements.

After President Lyndon Baines Johnson transferred the property to the Smithsonian in 1965, the Washington, DC, architect Hugh Newell Jacobsen began the arduous task of restoring the building to its original use as an art gallery. The restored building, renamed the Renwick Gallery and now a National Historic Landmark, was opened to the public in 1973. With the building once more filled with art, and the Grand Salon again hung salon style with tiers of pictures, the Renwick was returned to its earlier glory. "We want people to appreciate the architecture," said the first director, Lloyd Herman. "The building really is our own biggest exhibit."

In 2013 the Renwick underwent another extensive renovation, the first in more than forty years, overseen by Westlake Reed Leskosky. Two long-concealed vaulted ceilings were restored, along with numerous decorative features. An LED lighting system was one element of a highly effective upgrade of the mechanical systems, which reduced the building's energy usage by 70 percent, making the building one of the most efficient of all the Smithsonian museums. The restored spaces today showcase the latest in contemporary craft art.

Commissioned for the Renwick's 2015 reopening, the sinuous red carpet on the grand staircase is the creation of French architect Odile Decq.

NANCY BROWN NEGLEY HALL

The museum was originally housed in the Art Deco–style Carver Theater, designed by the Baltimore architect John Zink (1886–1952), who created more than four hundred theaters in the mid-Atlantic region.

Director John R. Kinard stands in front of the Anacostia Neighborhood Museum, now known as the Anacostia Community Museum, May 1968.

The Anacostia Community Museum, set in the lush woods of Fort Stanton Park on the east bank of the Anacostia River, in a historically Black neighborhood not far from the Capitol, has a unique place in the Smithsonian constellation. It was the first museum to be placed in a neighborhood, rather than with the other Smithsonian museums on the Mall. Shortly after he became secretary in 1964, S. Dillon Ripley sought a Smithsonian presence beyond the marble monuments of the institution's historic center on the National Mall, in order to take museums directly to new and underserved audiences. As the first director, community activist and pastor John Kinard, later explained: "Museums can no longer serve only the intellectually elite, the art connoisseur, and the scholar . . . we must begin where the people are."

The museum's first home was the Carver Theatre (1948, John J. Zink), which was named for George Washington Carver, a noted African American agricultural researcher and teacher. After being converted to museum use, the moderne-style movie theater was opened to the public as the Anacostia Neighborhood Museum on September 15, 1967. It quickly became a leading site for experimental, community-driven exhibitions, including a hands-on children's room that inspired Discovery Rooms at museums around the country. During its first year, the museum had more than eighty thousand visitors.

The award-winning Drumline of Garfield Prep Academy Elementary School performed in 2017 for the museum's fiftieth anniversary celebrations.

The main entrance of the museum, nestled in the woods of Fort Stanton Park, is notable for its cylinders inset with diamonds of glass block and blue tile.

The museum continued to attract visitors and soon outgrew its space in the theater. A new home in Fort Stanton Park was constructed in 1984, incorporating an existing metal building erected in 1973 as a storage facility for the museum. A brick addition to the structure, including exhibit space and offices, was designed by the Washington, DC, architecture firm Keyes Condon Florance.

In 2002 the museum undertook an unusual renovation, working with two design firms: architrave p.c. of Washington, for the public front facade, and Wisnewski Blair of Alexandria, Virginia, for the rear of the building. The two firms complemented each other well, creating a space that maximized the utility of the original building while adding features that speak to African American history. Large picture windows at the entrance and in the side galleries allow visitors ample views of the museum's leafy hilltop setting. The facade's use of red brick, in patterns suggesting a woven Kente cloth, draws on African inspiration. Flanking the entry, concrete cylinders pierced with glass block and blue tile evoke the conical towers of the eleventh-century city of Great Zimbabwe, one of the oldest and largest ancient structures in southern Africa.

Glass, metal, and brick define the rear of the two-story building, which is designed to hold offices and other support facilities. This service portion of the museum melds seamlessly with the more colorful front facade. Most of the 1973 metal building was demolished to provide new interior space, although traces of it can still be found in the exhibition area. The design won the 2002 Vision Award from one of Washington's oldest planning groups, the Committee of 100 on the Federal City, which cited the building as "an architectural tour de force symbolizing African crafts and design."

The museum was renamed the Anacostia Community Museum in 2006, reflecting the institution's historic focus. In 2019, the museum reopened after an extensive exterior and interior refurbishment. The redesigned landscape, featuring native plants, includes an urban garden and an installation about the Anacostia watershed—a critical aspect of the museum's multiyear initiative to explore citizen efforts to reclaim urban waterways.

A weathered-steel and stained-glass sculpture, entitled Real Justice: The Spirit of Thurgood Marshall (2004), is on loan from its sculptor, Allen Uzikee Nelson of Washington.

HIRSHHORN MUSEUM AND SCULPTURE GARDEN

Joseph Hirshhorn, whose modern art collection forms the core of the Hirshhorn Museum and Sculpture Garden, called his gift "a small repayment for what this nation has done for me and others like me who arrived here as immigrants. What I accomplished in the United States I could not have accomplished anywhere else in the world." The museum's opening in 1974 represented a landmark moment for modern art in the capital: the fulfillment of a longstanding desire for a national museum of modern and contemporary art on the Mall. Congress had passed legislation establishing one as early as the 1930s, and a design was actually drafted by the father-and-son team of Eliel (1873–1950) and Eero (1910–61) Saarinen. The sleek, functional museum they proposed was probably too avant-garde for Washington, however, and in any case plans for its execution were abandoned in the face of World War II.

Hirshhorn (1899–1981), who was born in Latvia and came to the United States as a child, was a mining entrepreneur and a self-taught art collector and patron. In the late 1940s he sold the impressionist paintings he had collected and began focusing on contemporary art and sculpture, amassing an unparalleled collection that included major works by Thomas Eakins, Auguste Rodin, Constantin Brancusi, Henri Matisse, and many artists whom Hirshhorn befriended, such as Willem de Kooning, Pablo Picasso, Edward Hopper, and Alberto Giacometti. His collection was exceptionally strong in sculpture, much of it displayed outdoors on the vast lawns of his Connecticut home.

The Hirshhorn was built on the site of the original Army Medical Museum (1886). Architect Gordon Bunshaft conceived the doughnut-shaped building as "a large piece of functional sculpture."

Hirshhorn's art collection became the subject of intense international interest after a 1962 exhibition at the Guggenheim Museum in New York City, with museums across the United States, as well as in Italy, Israel, and Canada, vying for it. S. Dillon Ripley, then the Smithsonian's secretary, and President Lyndon Baines Johnson, who invited the Hirshhorns to the White House, successfully pressed the collector to donate his art to the nation. In 1966 Congress passed an act establishing the museum, with an outdoor sculpture garden an integral part of the design from the beginning.

As its architect the Smithsonian chose Gordon Bunshaft (1909–90), the leading designer of Skidmore, Owings and Merrill. Bunshaft had made his reputation with the ground-breaking Lever House (1952) in New York City, but it was his luminous marble Beinecke Library (1963) at Yale University that especially caught Secretary Ripley's imagination. Faced with the challenge of situating the Hirshhorn amid the monuments of the Mall, Bunshaft developed a starkly modern design that was geometrical, monumental, and, above all, sculptural—like many of the works in the donor's collection. An art collector himself, Bunshaft had strong ideas about how contemporary art should be displayed. Primary in his thinking were circulation and space flow. The cylindrical form he chose was originally to be clad in Roman travertine marble, which would have provided some stylistic relationship with John Russell Pope's classical National Gallery of Art (1941) across the Mall. Because of budget constraints, the Hirshhorn Museum was built instead using precast concrete mixed with a crushed aggregate of pink granite.

Doug Aitken's SONG 1 *is a stunning use of the building's exterior as exhibit. Set to the song, "I Only Have Eyes for You," the work transformed the building into "liquid architecture" and an urban soundspace in the summer of 2012.*

The circular courtyard is centered on a fountain, visible to visitors through the windows above. Coffered ribs on the underside of the museum, illuminated at night, add drama to the design.

As with his Beinecke Library, which sits atop four pillars, Bunshaft envisioned the Hirshhorn floating above its plaza. Four massive piers were an essential aspect of the design. The architect drew attention to the sheer technical audacity of this feat by making the underside of the ring hold its own dramatic aesthetic interest, with deep concrete coffering creating a pattern of ribs. Bunshaft's elevated building left the plaza and the museum's nearly four-acre plot virtually open for the display and enjoyment of art. On the plaza, at the center of the ring, he placed a circular fountain, which became one of the building's signature features.

District of Columbia Mayor Walter Washington presents the keys to the city to a smiling Joseph Hirshhorn on October 4, 1974, the museum's opening day (left).

Escalators in the modernist glass lobby (below) whisk visitors up or down to the galleries. In 2018 artist Hiroshi Sugimoto transformed the modernist lobby into an immersive artwork, creating a new gathering space at the Smithsonian in the process.

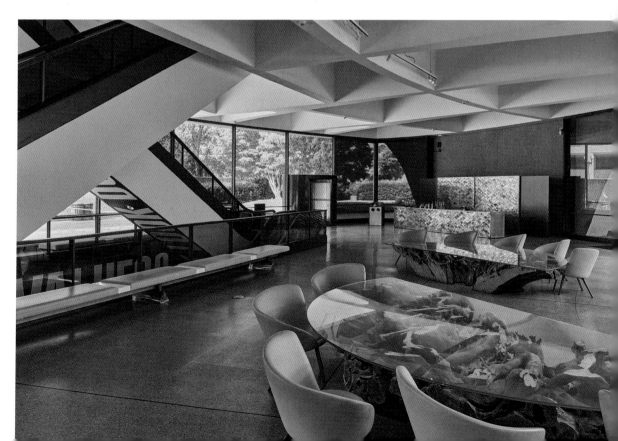

directions **Amy Sillman**
third person singular

The eighty-two-foot-tall building is entered from Independence Avenue through a glass lobby containing escalators to carry visitors up and down. A basement and three floors of public exhibition space above ground offer some sixty thousand square feet of exhibition area, while the top floor is reserved for staff offices. Galleries rim the museum's outer ring; an internal ovoid-shaped ring contains terrazzo-floored corridors, with sculpture displays and benches for visitors. The inner walls are curtains of glass that look out onto the central courtyard and the fountain. On the third floor a balcony offers a panoramic view of the Mall; from the exterior this appears as a thin, horizontal window, the only rupture in the facade's monumental severity.

The glass-walled gallery facing the courtyard often displays sculpture (opposite).

Barbara Kruger's Belief+Doubt installation fills the lower level, wrapping the entire space— walls, floor, and escalators— in text-printed vinyl phrases, which address questions of power, desire, and consumption.

New landscaping was added to the sculpture garden during its renovation in 1981. Visible here are Henry Moore's Draped Reclining Figure (1952–53, cast 1956), Dan Graham's For Gordon Bunshaft (2006, fabricated 2007–8), and on the upper level, Roy Lichtenstein's Brushstroke (1966).

Bunshaft wanted to emphasize the special location of the museum, halfway between the Washington Monument and the Capitol. The Hirshhorn lies at the southernmost end of a key north–south axis developed in L'Enfant's original plan for the city and reinforced in the 1901 McMillan Plan; this axis also takes in the National Gallery of Art's sculpture garden, the National Archives, and the Old Patent Office Building (today the Smithsonian American Art Museum and National Portrait Gallery). To underscore this axis, Bunshaft proposed a sunken sculpture garden running across the Mall, featuring a 350-foot-long reflecting pool surrounded by walkways and outdoor sculpture. Although the plan generated intense controversy over the possibility that the historic vista between the Capitol and the Washington Monument might be disrupted, it was approved by city and federal authorities. Tremendous public opposition developed, however, and plans for construction were halted.

The sculpture garden was eventually built as a much smaller sunken plot close to the museum, following a 1971 proposal by Benjamin Forgey, then the architecture critic of the *Washington Star*. The austere, pebble-surfaced garden was reconfigured in 1981 by the prominent landscape architect Lester Collins (1914–93), providing wheelchair access, lush areas of lawn, shade and ornamental trees, and additional plantings. The sculpture garden is due to be altered again by Japanese artist and architect Hiroshi Sugimoto, in order to accommodate both large- and small-scale sculptures as well as performing arts spaces. The plaza around the building was likewise redeveloped in 1993, with further plantings and raised parterres added by James Urban and Associates, a landscape design firm in Annapolis, Maryland. The building, fountain, and plaza are next scheduled for renovation in 2026.

The sculpture garden was not the only controversial aspect of the original Hirshhorn design. The building itself represented such a dramatic departure from earlier buildings on the Mall that it provoked extremely strong reactions at the time of its opening in 1974. While Paul Goldberger of the *New York Times* praised the circular plan and its "pleasant processional sequence," his famous colleague, Ada Louise Huxtable, called the building "born-dead, neo-penitentiary modern." Backlash also arose against the donor and the idea of erecting a memorial on the Mall to a living person. Yet as time passed, these controversies receded. In 1981 the *Washington Post* hailed the redesigned sculpture garden as a "jewel-like park within a park."

In its mission to explore and engage the arts and artists of today, the Hirshhorn Museum has greatly expanded on Joseph Hirshhorn's original bequest. The museum created a black-box space in the basement for exhibiting video and other new media art; it has commissioned many new pieces for its permanent collection, and it supports a wide range of temporary shows, experimental projects, and artist retrospectives. As Secretary Ripley said at the time of the opening, "The purpose of the Hirshhorn is to remind us all that life is more than the usual, that the human mind in its relentless diversity is capable of seeing life subjectively, and being stirred by objects into new and positive ways of thought, thus escaping from the numbing penumbra of the ritual known as everyday."

The Hirshhorn's stark geometry creates a streamlined backdrop for the bronze sculptural group Last Conversation Piece (1994–95), by Juan Muñoz.

NATIONAL AIR AND SPACE MUSEUM

The Air and Space Museum's marble-clad masses alternate with glass and steel-framed voids (opposite). The glass wall at the building's west end can be removed to accommodate the movement of large exhibit objects.

The National Air and Space Museum opened on July 1, 1976—as part of the Bicentennial of the United States—to thrilled visitors. A series of dramatic, alternating masses of marble and glass, the building features exhibition spaces that show airplanes suspended against the natural backdrop of the sky. "It's probably the only place in the world where people can walk through a real spacecraft," said the museum's first director, the Apollo 11 astronaut Michael Collins. At the dedication, President Gerald R. Ford declared the museum "America's birthday gift to itself." And the Washington Post heralded the opening as a "Bicentennial Blast-Off for a Wonder of Marble and Glass." The New York Times architecture critic, Ada Louise Huxtable, was more tongue-in-cheek when she wrote, "It's a bird, it's a plane, it's Supermuseum!" and called the museum "a cross between Disney World and the Cabinet of Dr. Caligari." The building and its contents continue to enthrall visitors today.

The Smithsonian has been collecting objects associated with flight ever since the tenure of its third secretary, Samuel P. Langley, an astronomer who competed (unsuccessfully) with the Wright Brothers in the quest for the first manned flight. Langley's Great Aerodrome of 1903, which was built in a shed in the South Yard behind the Castle, is now on display at the Air and Space Museum's Steven F. Udvar-Hazy Center. In 1928 Charles Lindbergh presented the institution with the world's most famous plane, the Spirit of St. Louis, and in 1948 the Wright Brothers' 1903 Flyer found its permanent home at the Smithsonian as well.

This 1917 Quonset hut in the South Yard behind the Castle, originally used by the US Signal Service, became the home of the National Air Museum's early air and space collection.

The only building large enough at the time to house these objects was the Arts and Industries Building; above the exhibits of presidential china and the like, planes were hung from the roof trusses as if in midflight. Once the space program began, rockets were given to the Smithsonian, and these—too large of course for the building—were displayed outside, along what became known as Rocket Row. Many of the air and space objects were also exhibited in an old World War I Quonset hut in the Castle's South Yard. In 1946 Congress formally established the National Air Museum. Twenty years later, as the space race captured the nation's imagination, Congress authorized $40 million for the construction of a major new building on the Mall to house the museum.

The Smithsonian awarded the commission to the St. Louis–based architecture firm Hellmuth Obata and Kassabaum for the challenging project—a building on the historic Mall that could handle both enormous objects and enormous crowds. Gyo Obata (b. 1923), the principal designer, studied for a time at the Cranbrook Academy of Art in Michigan under the Finnish architect Eliel Saarinen, whose son Eero designed Dulles International Airport (1962). "When I went to Cranbrook to study with Eliel Saarinen," Obata reminisced, "he taught me not to be afraid of large projects, of the planning involved and so forth. Learning about community, urban planning and the relationships of buildings to each other was a very important part of my learning and an important inspiration to me."

Alan B. Shepard Jr. examines the Freedom 7 spacecraft after his Project Mercury suborbital flight in 1961. The craft was then located in the National Air Museum in the South Yard behind the Castle.

Obata was challenged to design a museum near the foot of the Capitol that would fit in with the classical grandeur of the Mall, while creating an architectural statement that reflected the modernity of space exploration. The architect carefully studied the axial relationship of the site to the National Gallery of Art's original building and the Hirshhorn Museum. By varying the massing, the design "prevented an overly monolithic effect," he noted, adding that the blocks' "recesses align with projecting portions of the National Gallery's south elevation as if the buildings might fit together like two pieces of a puzzle." His 636,000-square-foot building comprised four sections clad in the same Tennessee marble used for the National Gallery's West Building. The marble alternated between glass in three recessed exhibit bays; flooded with even, north-facing light, these glass areas featured heavy truss systems to support the planes suspended above. Window walls were placed at each end of the building as portals to bring in large artifacts; the one at the west end is still active. The building's large-format IMAX theater was the first one built in Washington, DC.

In 1988 the museum returned to the original architects to design a large glass pavilion for a restaurant at the building's east end. In 2000 the building's skylights, which had been executed in acrylic plastic as a cost-cutting measure, were replaced with glass, as Obata had intended. At the same time, the museum's window glass was replaced with slightly tinted glass to better protect the objects. New perimeter vestibules were also added to the north and south entrances, providing an extra layer of climate control between the outside elements and the exhibits.

In conjunction with the fortieth anniversary of the museum in 2016, the museum restored its iconic Milestones of Flight gallery. Three years later the museum began a massive, phased renovation led by Quinn Evans Architects. The mechanical systems are being updated, and the original marble veneer panels, which were deteriorating, are being replaced with colonial rose granite cladding. A soaring, new wing-shaped entrance will also be added to the north (Mall) side of the building.

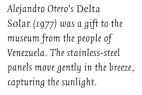

Alejandro Otero's Delta Solar (1977) was a gift to the museum from the people of Venezuela. The stainless-steel panels move gently in the breeze, capturing the sunlight.

Several sculptures grace the grounds of the museum and are an important element of the museum's overall appearance. *Delta Solar*, a triangular stainless-steel sculpture evoking sails, created by the renowned Venezuelan artist Alejandro

Otero (1921–90), is set in a water feature at the west end of the building. Facing the Mall at the museum's south entrance is *Continuum*, a work depicting the cosmos by the American sculptor Charles O. Perry (1929–2011). The third sculpture, at the north entrance, is by Richard Lippold (1915–2002): *Ad Astra* (Latin for "to the stars"), notable for its delicate starbursts and slim vertical tapers. The artworks—evoking images of rockets, jet streams, wings, antennae satellites, planes, balloons, gliders, and other air and space vehicles—hint at the collections that await visitors inside. Within the museum, the history of space exploration is captured by *The Space Mural: A Cosmic View*, by Robert T. McCall (1919–2010).

The National Air and Space Museum remains one of the most popular in the world. In 2007 *Architectural Record* and the Harris Interactive Poll named it one of America's one hundred favorite buildings, and in 2018, seven million visitors made this the most popular museum in the Smithsonian collection. But as airplanes and spacecraft grew exponentially larger than the vehicles from the dawn of the space age, the need arose in the late twentieth century for larger quarters in which to display them. No land was available on the Mall or in downtown Washington, so the Smithsonian ventured out to Fairfax County, Virginia, for a twenty-first-century–sized facility.

As part of a multiphased renovation, the museum is gaining a striking new entrance on the Mall. Designed with a paraboloid roof suggesting flight, the climatized vestibule provides shelter to visitors as they wait to pass through security screening to enter the museum.

At the center of the museum is the popular Boeing Milestones of Flight Hall. The glass curtain wall and the skylights offer the sky as a backdrop for the aircraft. Charles Lindbergh's Spirit of St. Louis, the Apollo Lunar Module LM-2, and SpaceShipOne, the first privately developed piloted vehicle to reach space, are among the objects on view.

Rockets on display in the museum are easily accommodated in the vast interior galleries (opposite). Viewing platforms and stairs allow visitors to see from all angles.

STEVEN F. UDVAR-HAZY CENTER

To develop the Steven F. Udvar-Hazy Center as part of the National Air and Space Museum, the Smithsonian returned once more to Helmuth Obata and Kassabaum. This facility in Chantilly, Virginia, nestled between the eighteenth-century Sully Plantation and Eero Saarinen's mid-twentieth-century Dulles International Airport, houses the largest aviation and space artifacts in the Air and Space collection. Named in honor of its major donor, who is the owner of one of the world's largest aircraft-leasing companies, it opened in December 2003.

The mammoth Udvar-Hazy Center contains four main components: the barrel-ceilinged Boeing Aviation Hangar, the James S. McDonnell Space Hanger, the Mary Baker Engen Restoration Hangar, and a 164-foot-high observation tower; the latter, reminiscent of an airport control tower, is named in memory of Donald D. Engen, who died in a gliding accident in 1999 while he was director of the Air and Space Museum. In addition to approximately 2,800 aviation-related artifacts, more than one thousand space artifacts, and several dozen art objects, Udvar-Hazy also contains a 479-seat IMAX theater, classrooms, offices, and visitor amenities. The center's landscaping includes the sculptural *Space Exploration Wall of Honor* outside the building's main entrance and the seventy-foot work *Ascent*, by the Virginia sculptor John Safer (1922–2018).

An aerial view of the Steven F. Udvar-Hazy Center of the National Air and Space Museum (above) shows the entire complex and reveals how one section interlocks with another.

John Safer's Ascent, located at the end of a walkway honoring those with a passion for flight (opposite), welcomes visitors to the museum.

Taut, brushed-steel cladding resembling aircraft skin covers Udvar-Hazy (below). The Donald D. Engen Observation Tower provides views of air traffic at nearby Dulles Airport, and the circular form behind it houses an IMAX theater.

A side view of the Boeing Aviation Hangar reveals the wide doors that open to move large aircraft. The structure recalls the enormous dirigible hangars built by the US Navy at the start of World War II.

The Boeing Aviation Hangar, which encompasses nearly three hundred thousand square feet, recalls the immense hangars constructed in the early twentieth century to house dirigibles. It is so enormous that the entire National Air and Space Museum on the Mall could fit inside it. The aircraft on exhibit, suspended from twenty-one steel trusses (each of which holds up to twenty thousand pounds), can be viewed from several vantage points: on the ground and at eye level on a series of catwalks surrounding the hangar. "When we hang the craft, we try to show them in positions or at angles that capture their spirit or purpose," explains William "Jake" Jacobs, an exhibit designer. Air ducts are cleverly curved to blend with the trusses, and the railings around the exhibit areas and catwalks of both hangars are punctuated at intervals by benches, so visitors can rest and enjoy the space. To protect the artifacts, both the aviation and space hangars were designed using a minimum of natural light. The Boeing Hanger is illuminated by a clerestory window, while the 53,067-square-foot James S. McDonnell Space Hangar, which contains the 1976 space shuttle Enterprise, has a darkened ceiling evocative of outer space.

For conservation of the Smithsonian's air and space artifacts, the museum opened a new wing in 2011, consolidating in one state-of-the-art facility operations that had taken place at a storage facility in Suitland, Maryland, since the 1950s. The new hangar, a gift of the Engen family, is named in honor of the wife of the late naval aviator and NASM director Donald Engen. With the Mary Baker Engen Restoration Hangar, the Udvar-Hazy Center covers approximately 760,000 square feet. Visitors can see restoration work in progress, as well as more of the Air and Space Museum's collections than have ever been shown before.

Samuel P. Langley's Great Aerodrome (1903) is suspended from the roof of the Udvar-Hazy Center as if in flight (left).

The Concorde, donated by Air France, fits easily into the mammoth Boeing Aviation Hangar (below). Suspended walkways provide an eye-level view of the exhibits.

COOPER HEWITT,
SMITHSONIAN DESIGN MUSEUM

The Cooper-Hewitt's campus on Manhattan's Upper East Side (opposite) occupies Andrew Carnegie's Georgian-style mansion, along with its spacious garden, and two townhouses on East Ninetieth Street, visible here in the foreground.

In 1976 the Smithsonian opened a museum devoted to design in the former New York City home of the steel magnate and philanthropist Andrew Carnegie (1835–1919). The Upper East Side mansion, the namesake of its neighborhood, the Carnegie Hill Historic District, is now home to a collection of more than 215,000 objects—ranging from textiles and wall coverings to drawings, prints, applied arts, and furniture. Carnegie's daughter, Margaret, suggested that her father's "heart would sing" to know that his home was open to the public.

The mansion was designed at the turn of the twentieth century in the style of a Georgian country house by the New York architecture firm Babb, Cook and Willard. The architects were known for their grand residential estates on Long Island, as well as for office buildings such as Montreal's first skyscraper, the New York Life Insurance Building (1887). Carnegie, unlike other wealthy architecture patrons such as the Astors and the Vanderbilts, told his architects that he desired "the most modest, plainest and roomiest house in New York." The location he selected, on northern Fifth Avenue, was then considered by fashionable society to be almost wilderness, but it provided his wife, Louise, and their new baby with ample space for a garden. Construction began in 1901, the year Carnegie sold his Carnegie Steel Company to the United States Steel Corporation. He devoted the rest of his life to giving away his fortune, founding the Carnegie Corporation in the mansion. He focused especially on establishing free public libraries in the United States and his native Scotland.

Louis Comfort Tiffany's influence is visible in the scalloped-glass canopy at the main entrance to the Cooper-Hewitt Museum.

The sixty-four-room house, built at a cost $1 million, may not have been modest or plain, but it certainly was roomy, and it incorporated modern technology. Although the four-story building appears to be built of brick with limestone trim, it actually features a structural steel frame. Steel skeletons were making possible the earliest skyscrapers at this time; Carnegie's mansion was one of the first private residences in New York City to use this pioneering technology—a choice that was especially fitting, given that Carnegie had made his fortune in steel. The house had one of the first residential Otis passenger elevators (now in the Smithsonian's National Museum of American History), and it also boasted an artesian well, its own generator, and a sophisticated humidification, heating, and air-conditioning system.

Large fans in the attic pulled air in from outside through filters in the basement, over tanks of cooling water, and then into every room. Brass-and-copper coal-fueled boilers manufactured by Babcock and Wilcox, the country's leading boiler company (which was at that time installing the boilers to power New York's new subway system), were housed in a hygienic white-tiled room. Still visible today are the miniature railroad tracks on which the coal car traveled to convey fuel from the 250-ton coal bin to the furnace.

A grand paneled stair, illuminated by an early electric light fixture by Edward F. Caldwell, leads from the main entrance to the second floor.

The house is entered through a portico with a bronze and leaded-glass canopy, designed in the style of Louis Comfort Tiffany. Past the marble vestibule, the main hall and ceiling are paneled in Scottish oak, in deference to Carnegie's ancestry, and the parquet floor (now replaced) was a rare, tropical monkey wood. Every morning the Carnegies were awakened by the sound of the organist Walter C. Gale performing on the house's enormous Aeolian organ. Once a centerpiece of the main hall, it was removed when the Smithsonian took over the building. Carnegie loved the instrument so much that he donated more than eight thousand organs to churches, civic institutions, and schools. The first floor contained the main suite of entertaining rooms: a parlor, a formal drawing room, and a dining room, as well as the family's breakfast room and a glass conservatory. The west end of this floor, overlooking Central Park, was given over to Andrew Carnegie's library and office. Carnegie, who was five feet two inches tall, specified that the doors in this area be a full foot shorter than those in the rest of the house to ensure that his visitors accommodate themselves to his diminutive perspective.

A grand Scottish-oak stair leads to the second floor, which once housed the Carnegie family's bedrooms, dressing rooms, and sitting rooms. The library, distinguished from the rest of the house by its ornately carved, Indian-style teakwood decoration, was designed by the noted plein-air painter and interior designer Lockwood de Forest (1850–1932); de Forest set up a studio in Ahmedabad, India, run by Muggunbhai Hutheesing, where master craftsmen created the carved

panels for export to the US. The rooms on this floor are now all exhibition galleries. They retain many of their original architectural features, such as carved mantels, plasterwork, and elaborate wood door surrounds. The third floor featured guest rooms, a suite for Mrs. Carnegie's sister, a schoolroom for daughter Margaret, and a gym for Andrew. The fourth floor housed quarters for twenty-five or more servants, most from Scotland, who worked for the family. Today these upper floors provide a variety of expanded gallery areas and support spaces.

All of the house's principal rooms were designed to face the large garden at the rear, which was the pride of Louise Carnegie. Surrounded by a wrought-iron fence and stone posts, it contained azaleas, wisteria, rhododendrons, crab apple and chestnut trees, and a rock garden she designed herself. There was even a playhouse for Margaret.

After Carnegie died in 1919, his widow continued to live in the house until her death in 1946. It was then turned over to the Carnegie Corporation and leased to the Columbia University School of Social Work, which undertook renovations to adapt it for use as a school. In 1963, the Cooper Union for the Advancement of Science and Art announced its intention to disband its museum (which had been founded in 1897 by the granddaughters of the industrialist Peter Cooper). Hundreds joined a campaign to save the collection, and in 1967 the Smithsonian stepped in to make the newly named Cooper Hewitt Museum part of the national collection. Carnegie Corporation offered the mansion as a home for the new museum, at first leasing it and then in 1972 donating it, along with an adjacent townhouse on East Ninetieth Street that had been the home of the Carnegies' daughter. Secretary S. Dillon Ripley spoke at the time of "the need for a museum showcase, in which an endlessly rich variety of historical decorative arts material can be drawn upon, utilized and enjoyed." He proposed that "the Smithsonian can be influential in offering guidelines to more beautiful designs in everyday life."

Many of the elaborate decorative features of the Gilded Age mansion remain, including the stained-glass tympanum window that overlooks the garden (above, left). In the gallery that was once the Carnegies' drawing room, each corner of the coved plaster ceiling features musical instruments (above, right).

The mansion's historic spaces showcase objects from the extensive collections as well as contemporary design. For this 2019–20 exhibition (above), the Wyss Institute at Harvard University selected permanent collection works on a theme of biofuturism.

One of the most spectacular rooms in the Carnegie's mansion was the family's library on the second floor (opposite). Lockwood de Forest distinguished its design with Indian-style carved teak-wood decoration and stencil ornament. This 2016–17 exhibition featured works by Louis Comfort Tiffany, the artist who produced the original room's lamps and chandelier.

The museum faces many challenges in displaying within the confines of a historic house a growing collection dedicated to design. To provide additional space for offices, classrooms, and other programmatic uses, the museum acquired a second townhouse at 11 East Ninetieth Street in 1989. In 1996 the Cooper Hewitt hired Polshek and Partners (now Ennead Architects) to update the campus and make it more accessible. In addition to adapting the museum's front entrance, the architects renovated the adjacent townhouses and designed a connector (the Agnes Bourne Bridge Gallery) to link them to the mansion, using a style reminiscent of a garden pergola.

Another major, three-year renovation, completed by Gluckman Mayner Architects and Beyer Blinder Belle Architects and Planners LLP in 2014, gave the museum its first open "white box" space on the third floor, greatly increasing the exhibition space in the building. The historic spaces on the first two floors were conserved, and the mansion's garden entrance was made accessible as well. National Design Award winner Walter Hood was engaged to reimagine The Arthur Ross Terrace and Garden, which now opens to the street, inviting the community to enjoy this oasis in the city.

THE QUADRANGLE

The elegant Enid A. Haupt Garden sits in the center of the Quadrangle complex, bounded by some of the Smithsonian's most historic buildings: the Castle, the Arts and Industries Building, and the Freer Gallery of Art. It spreads across 4.2 acres, with courts and contemplative corners designed to evoke a traditional Persian garden, a Chinese water garden, and an ornate Victorian parterre—creating a dialogue between East and West. Despite its grandeur, it is in a sense only a roof garden. Beneath this placid scene is an immense sunken structure housing the National Museum of African Art, the Arthur M. Sackler Gallery, and the S. Dillon Ripley Center. Three separate pavilions in the garden lead to the two underground museums and the education center.

The collection of the African Art Museum was amassed by Warren M. Robbins (1923–2008), a Foreign Service officer, who displayed it beginning in 1964 in a Capitol Hill rowhouse where Frederick Douglass had once resided. Robbins

In a 1984 construction photograph, workers are shown laying concrete underground. Extreme care was taken to protect the Smithsonian's three nearby historic structures—the Castle, the Arts and Industries Building, and the Freer Gallery of Art.

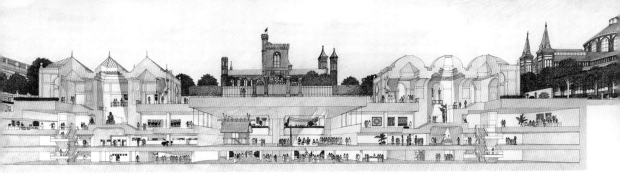

founded the museum to teach Americans the value of African art and culture. Now a leading center for the study and display of ancient and contemporary African visual arts, it became a part of the Smithsonian by a 1979 act of Congress. The Sackler Gallery, together with the Freer, forms the National Museum of Asian Art. It was named for Arthur M. Sackler (1913–87), the pharmaceutical research scientist and marketing executive whose 1982 gift to the Smithsonian included a thousand outstanding Asian and Near Eastern works of art and funding for a building.

The desire to place the Sackler Gallery next to the Freer, coupled with the lack of open space on the Mall, drove the selection of the utilitarian South Yard behind the Castle as the site for the new museum complex. The Quadrangle opened to the public in 1987, following a complicated planning, design, and construction phase lasting nine years. Recalling a historic design feature of many English and American colleges and universities, the Quadrangle also reflects in its name Secretary Ripley's vision for the Smithsonian as a university open to all the world—a place for scholars, students, artists, and families to come together.

A number of architects and landscape architects contributed to the Quadrangle. In 1978 the Japanese architect Junzo Yoshimura (1908–97), a figure greatly admired by American art patrons and revered in his own country, developed the concept of a discreet building located within and largely under a garden. Shepley, Bulfinch, Richardson and Abbott (today Shepley Bulfinch), the oldest continuously operating American architecture firm, was retained in 1980 to shepherd the project through the historic preservation and design review process and to oversee construction.

In response to comments by the US Commission of Fine Arts and the National Capital Planning Commission, Jean-Paul Carlhian (1919–2012), principal architect for Shepley Bulfinch, significantly reworked the design. He recast the project to harmonize the new facilities with the existing landmark buildings of the Mall. From the strong colors and Victorian skylines of the Castle and the Arts and Industries Building, he developed the pyramidal roofs of the Sackler Gallery and the reddish hue of the African Art Museum. From the arch and wave motifs of the limestone Freer Gallery, he adopted the warm gray granite color of the Sackler and the rounded domes of African Art. The third garden structure, a round, pagoda-like pavilion that provides the entrance to the Ripley Center, was adapted from a drawing by the English garden designer Humphry Repton (1752–1818).

The Quadrangle complex, as shown in this architectural rendering, is almost fully underground, except for the entrance pavilions to the three facilities. The Sackler Gallery, the African Art Museum, and the S. Dillon Ripley Center can be accessed from the lowest (third) level without going outside.

Nearly 96 percent of the Quadrangle lies underground. The engineering and design were extremely challenging, because one-third of the complex sits below the city's water table. Concrete slurry walls, a construction technique developed in Carlhian's native France, were used to build the foundations. The engineers had to account for the weight of the garden's several feet of damp earth and its cast-concrete water features.

The round domes of the African Art Museum's entrance pavilion were inspired in part by African architectural forms as well as by the round arches of the Freer Gallery across the Quadrangle.

Great care was taken to create a graceful descent into the underground facilities. The pavilion entrances have soaring ceilings and huge windows that frame vistas of the garden and the Castle. Carlhian wanted to avoid the association of going down into a "bargain basement" or an underground garage, so he suffused the stairways of the two museums with light from stained-glass windows—amber for the Sackler and blue for African Art—as well as from clear glass skylights in the roof. Each stairway was given its own distinctive design, echoing the forms of the roofs— curved for African Art and diamond-shaped for the Sackler. And at the bottom of each stair is a sparkling water effect, reflecting the light from above.

Circular and octagonal motifs abound in the African Art Museum's postmodernist design, as seen especially in the central double stairway (opposite).

The Sackler entrance pavilion, shown here with a portrait of the Empress Dowager Cixi painted by American artist Katherine A. Carl in 1903, is often the site of contemporary art installations.

The entrance to the Ripley Center is a small kiosk (above) leading to the sprawling complex beneath.

A trompe-l'oeil mural by Richard Haas in the underground concourse (opposite) imagines classical ruins leading to the Arts and Industries Building.

The limestone spiral stairway for the entrance pavilion to the Ripley Center is a postmodern take on the monumental spiral stair of the Renaissance chateau of Blois in France. Halfway down, the visitor arrives at a shallow circular space lined with short, swelling columns, where the path swings around toward the concourse. Deliberately low and dark, this domed vestibule offers a dramatic contrast to the soaring, light-filled concourse below that serves all facilities. Lined with abstract classical motifs and crossed by bridges three stories above, this hall directs visitors to exhibitions and numerous classrooms.

The Moongate Garden (above), a postmodern take on the Temple of Heaven in Beijing, was conceived as an extension of the Sackler Gallery.

The colorful parterre in front of the south entrance of the Castle (opposite, above) pays homage to the 1976 Victorian Garden that preceded it.

Although the original architect of the Castle, James Renwick, designed these gates in the mid-nineteenth century, they were not built until 1987. Carved from local Seneca sandstone by Constantine Seferlis, the Renwick Gates provide an elegant entrance to the Haupt Garden (opposite).

The Haupt Garden is a remarkable oasis in the city, a far cry from the days when the South Yard contained work sheds and a parking lot. Enid A. Haupt (1906–2005), the publishing heiress and horticulture patron who funded it, requested mature specimen trees, saying that she was "getting on" and wanted to be able to enjoy the garden personally. The landscape designer Lester Collins (who was also involved in the reworking of the Hirshhorn Sculpture Garden) was brought in to consult on the plant selection. The African Art section features water effects evocative of North African–influenced designs in Andalusia. The Sackler garden, with its pink granite moon gates, was inspired by the Temple of Heaven in Beijing. The central parterre replicates the Victorian garden created behind the Castle for the Bicentennial in 1976. Nineteenth-century lampposts and the Smithsonian's collection of historic cast-iron garden furniture, urns, and wickets are scattered throughout the garden. The red sandstone gates at the Independence Avenue entrance to the garden are based on James Renwick's unexecuted original design; they were carved by Constantine Seferlis (1930–2005), a Greek-born stone carver who also worked on the Washington National Cathedral. Marrying old and new, the Renwick gates provide an elegant entryway to the hidden treasures of the Quadrangle complex.

NATIONAL POSTAL MUSEUM

The National Postal Museum occupies the building that originally served as the city's main post office building. Situated adjacent to Union Station, the monumental structure features an Ionic colonnade along its front facade.

The National Postal Museum opened in 1993 in the imposing Beaux-Arts building just off the Mall that for almost all of the twentieth century served as the main post office for the city of Washington. Depressions in the lobby floor, where people stood in line at the teller windows, are still visible. Completed in 1914, the post office was designed by the firm of Daniel Burnham of Chicago. Burnham, who died in 1912, was also responsible for the adjacent Union Station, which had opened in 1908. These buildings formed part of a monumental three-part composition that the architect envisioned as a classical entranceway to the

capital, centered on Union Station. The third building, meant to frame the train station on the eastern side—as the post office does on the western side—was finally built in 1992: the Thurgood Marshall Federal Judiciary Building, designed by Edward Larrabee Barnes (1915–2004).

At the beginning of the twentieth century, train travel dominated the country's transportation system. It was also the most efficient means of delivering the mail. Placing the post office next to the station meant that the two could be linked easily by rail, speeding up the processing of mail. In towns all across the nation, post offices were being similarly situated near railroad stations.

The neoclassical architecture of Burnham's post office building reflects the City Beautiful movement, which dominated American design in the early twentieth century. The movement had its origins in the monumental neoclassical buildings of Chicago's World's Columbian Exposition of 1893, the so-called White City. Under Burnham, Washington, DC, became one of the great exemplars of this progressive movement; he headed the McMillan Commission of 1901, which reimagined the Mall as a grand open space, harkening back to L'Enfant's original plan for the city. Burnham also helped design the dome of the Smithsonian's Natural History Museum, which was intended to serve as a stylistic model for future buildings in the capital.

By the 1950s, the original post office interior had been heavily modernized to suit the times. Fluorescent lighting replaced the marble torchères, plastic laminate countertops were added, and a low ceiling was installed to create a mezzanine for air-conditioning ducts and other utilities, destroying much of the original coffered ceiling in the lobby. Today this grand space has been restored with the reconstruction of the coffered ceiling and the ornamental plasterwork, the installation of replica chandeliers, and replacement of the torchères (now in bronze rather than marble), all of which provide an impressive setting for the entrance to the National Postal Museum.

The museum, which has one of the largest collections of stamps in the world, was created in 1990 by an agreement between the Smithsonian and the US Postal Service. It had its origins in the National Philatelic Collection, which was started at the Smithsonian in 1886 and first housed at the Arts and Industries Building and later at the National Museum of American History.

The museum exhibitions are located in the area behind the public lobby. This part of the building, once the mail-processing and distribution section, was never seen by the public visiting the city post office. The Washington-based firm Florance Eichbaum Esocoff King was the architect for the museum part of the building renovation. (The renovation of the entire building, which is managed by the US General Services Administration, was undertaken by the local architect Shalom Baranes.) The building itself still houses government offices.

Large-scale reproductions of postage stamps from the collection, illuminated at night, provide a semi-transparent decorative element on the south windows.

Many postal-themed elements were incorporated into the museum's interior design. The baluster detail on the escalators takes its inspiration from a cancellation mark. A silkscreened stamp design, featuring the famous 1901 Empire Express upside-down stamp, appears on the entrance hall ceiling. In the principal, central space of the museum are envelope-design tiles in the flooring and light fixtures that recall the rural towers once used by postal pilots to make mail drops. The William H. Gross Stamp Gallery, designed by Quinn Evans and opened in 2013, added extensive exhibition space and a new entrance off Massachusetts Avenue NW. The repurposing of this building as a museum has created a brilliant setting for the stories told here about the creation of the postal system and the movement of the mail in the United States.

The exhibit Moving the Mail, featuring a replica of a postal railway car, as well as mail planes and a stagecoach, sits in the atrium space that once served as the sorting area of the original post office.

National Museum
of the American Indian

Best known for the expressive, undulating building that opened on the Mall in 2004, the National Museum of the American Indian (NMAI) is actually housed in three architecturally distinct buildings in three locations. In 1989 Congress authorized the creation of this museum in Washington, DC, as part of the Smithsonian complex. The act stipulated that the collection of the Museum of the American Indian in New York City, which had been founded seven decades earlier by George Gustav Heye, be transferred to the Smithsonian. Because the museum was an important part of New York's cultural history, the Smithsonian agreed to retain a presence in the city, while moving the Heye collection to Washington. In New York the museum, which needed new quarters, was established in the historic Alexander Hamilton US Custom House at Bowling Green, near the foot of Manhattan. In the Washington area, two new buildings were planned: a prominent museum on the Mall and a structure dedicated to housing and caring for the collection in suburban Suitland, Maryland.

The designs for the two new buildings needed to embody the museum's mission: to advance knowledge and understanding of Native cultures of the Western hemisphere—past, present, and future—through partnership with Native people and others. It was important to involve Native peoples in every aspect of the design process and to try to encompass a great diversity of traditions and history, all while contending with a complex and conservative regulatory environment in the capital's historic core.

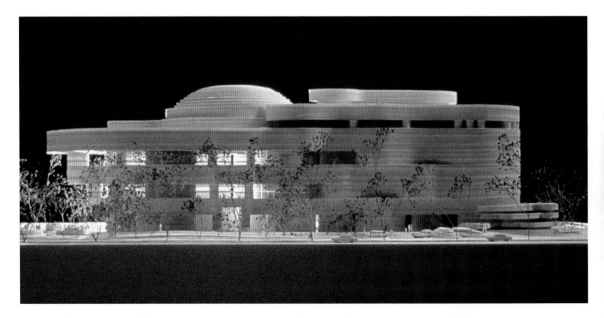

The design process for the National Museum of the American Indian on the Mall was unlike that undertaken for any previous Smithsonian museum. Douglas Cardinal (b. 1934), a member of the Canadian Blackfoot tribe, partnered with the Philadelphia architecture firm Geddes Brecher Qualls Cunningham for the project. Cardinal organized a three-day "vision session" in Washington in 1995, inviting tribal elders, who blessed the site of the future museum, as well as Native artists and others. Critical design ideas emerged from the session—for example, the building's entrance should face east, toward the rising sun; the museum should contain as much natural material as possible; it should acknowledge the four cardinal directions; and it should be welcoming to everyone. Cardinal believed that the new building "should endeavor to be a spiritual act and should demand from all those contributing to the design and construction the very best of their endeavors." He assembled a Native team to work with him on the design, among them an architect and landscape architect, Johnpaul Jones (Choctaw/Cherokee); an ethnobotanist, Donna House (Diné/Oneida); and a textile artist, Ramona Sakiestewa (Hopi).

The final building exudes an organic warmth, its curving walls drawn from studies of earth and rock formations eroded by time. The facade's rough-hewn Kasota limestone, which contains fossils in the blocks nearest the base, gradually becomes smoother as it reaches the top of the building. Constructed with an interior of poured-in-place concrete slabs, the 443,000-square-foot structure is five stories above grade, with a basement. The main entrance on the east end is framed with steel trusses that cantilever outward to form a dramatic protective canopy. This end of the building carries out a compelling dialogue with the Capitol, which it faces, including the Capitol's topmost statue *Freedom* (1863, Thomas Crawford), which wears a Native American headdress. A low, stepped dome on the museum complements the dome of the National Gallery of Art across the Mall. Its oculus, which opens up to the sky to bring in sunlight, serves as an interior focal point above the museum's central gathering space, called the Potomac (the Piscataway word for "Where the goods are brought in").

The exterior landscaping is a crucial part of the museum and is designed to invite visitors to return to a Native place and honor the Native hosts of the region on whose land the museum is built. The gardens include approximately 150 species of plants that are both indigenous to the region, from before European contact, and ethnobotanical, meaning they can be used for food, fiber, dye, medicine, building materials, and ceremonies. Water, an important element referencing the old Tiber Creek, flows around three sides of the building. Marking the cardinal points of the grounds are four enormous boulders, brought from four corners of the western hemisphere (Canada, Maryland, Chile, and Hawaii). Forty additional granite boulders from Canada, called "Grandfather Rocks"— the elders of the landscape, surround the museum.

The National Native American Veterans Memorial (opposite and below), which recognizes the tradition of service of Native Americans in every branch of the military, was designed by Harvey Pratt (Cheyenne/Arapaho), himself a veteran who served in Vietnam. Installed in 2020, the memorial incorporates water for cleansing and healing, benches for gathering and reflection, and four lances where visitors can leave prayer ties.

The design of this copper-screen wall acknowledges the Native weaving traditions of basketry and textiles. The spiral pattern is a solar reference. The screen's designer, Ramona Sakiestewa, a Hopi weaver from Santa Fe, New Mexico, also created the color schemes for the museum's interiors.

Throughout the exterior and the interior, the circle is a dominant form: the building is geometrically complex with more than a thousand curves and almost no straight walls. Each design element emphasizes an aspect of Native American traditions. The Potomac, the building's welcoming center, is full of architectural symbolism. The floor is laid with a circle of local red Seneca sandstone (the same material used for the Castle), surrounded by a ring of granite and maple flooring, all of which is set in quadrants and separated by metal strips aligned with the directions of the compass. A south-facing prism window captures sunlight, projecting patterns of color on the floor and walls. A copper screen wall referencing Navajo weaving traditions wraps around the area. All of the interior spaces use colors and themes from Native landscapes and decorative motifs reflecting indigenous environments and cultures.

The oculus in the ceiling above the Potomac, the 140-foot-high gathering place at the museum, emphasizes the importance of the sky to Native American cultures. A flowing staircase echoes the building's undulating forms (opposite).

Douglas Cardinal left the project before construction began in 1999, but his Native design team continued to work with Polshek and Partners (Ennead), SmithGroup, Jones and Jones, and the Native American Design Collaborative to finish the building. Consultations with Native Americans continued throughout the construction process. To celebrate the opening of this living museum, the building was launched in September 2004 with a week of festivities, attended by more than twenty thousand Native Americans from across North and South America, as well as some sixty-five thousand non-Natives.

The first of the two Washington-area buildings to be designed and built was actually the Cultural Resources Center, conceived to house the Heye collection of artifacts from New York, as well as to provide conservation facilities, traditional care, community consultation, and a research center. It is located within the Smithsonian's Suitland Collections Center campus in nearby Suitland, Maryland, a wooded area that includes a number of greenhouses and storage and conservation facilities, including the Smithsonian's Museum Support Center. The architecture firm Polshek and Partners (today Ennead Architects) of New York City (responsible for the 1996 renovation of the Cooper Hewitt, Smithsonian Design Museum) was selected to design the new structure in partnership with the Native American Design Collaborative and Tobey and Davis. Construction of the 164,000-square-foot building began in 1996 and was completed in fall 1998. Its radial steel roof in a nautilus shape references many indigenous and natural forms, such as the wing of a butterfly or a spider's web.

Because the collection contains many objects sacred to Native Americans, with different tribal customs for their handling, it was important that this new facility be a place that would not only store the objects using proper climate controls but also respect the objects' significant role in Native life. Special handling areas and ceremonial spaces are located both outside and inside, for use by staff and Native visitors. The CRC is also the home of NMAI's repatriation program and a center for community engagement and cultural exchange. Staff describe the Suitland center as the heart and soul of the museum, a place where the collections have found a respectful home.

The curving roof of the Cultural Resources Center reaches a dramatic apex at the northwest corner of the building (opposite). Native plantings surround the building, which is adjacent to a wooded area on two sides, north and east.

This model of the Cultural Resources Center in Suitland, Maryland (below, left), reveals the building's unusual roof, one of the first elements that emerged from a design workshop with the architects.

At the entrance to the Cultural Resources Center (below right), the building's solid steel roof becomes a glass-filled fretwork canopy.

The National Museum of the American Indian in New York City (right) is located at the foot of Manhattan in the 1899 building designed by architect Cass Gilbert as the US Customs House.

The Museum Store (below) includes the original light fixtures and decorative grilles from when this space was the cashier's office of the Custom House.

GEORGE GUSTAV HEYE CENTER (NMAI-NY)

When the new National Museum of the American Indian was authorized in 1989, the Alexander Hamilton US Custom House—a National Historic Landmark Beaux-Arts building completed in 1907—lay vacant and crumbling. Designed by architect Cass Gilbert (1859–1934), the 450,000-square-foot structure is a symphony of ornament and architectural detail. The entrance is flanked by the figures *The Four Continents*, by Daniel Chester French (1850–1931), sculptor of the seated Abraham Lincoln in the Lincoln Memorial. The building's interior contains many surprises, such as Guastavino-tile vaulting (like that found at the National Museum of Natural History), 1937 murals of New York Harbor by the Works Progress Administration artist Reginald Marsh (1898–1954), and sumptuous spaces indicative of the building's former use as the headquarters of the Port of New York. The building had been saved from the wrecking ball in 1979 by Senator Daniel Patrick Moynihan of New York but lacked a good use. The need to find a New York presence for the new American Indian Museum offered a solution. The General Services Administration leased the basement and the first and second floors to the Smithsonian, and the New York architecture firm Ehrenkrantz, Eckstut & Kuhn worked with the institution to design the space and conduct a complete exterior and interior restoration.

The Diker Pavilion for Native Arts and Cultures opened in 2006. Echoing the building's central rotunda on the floor above, the elliptical-shaped space is a program, exhibit, and special event space with glass exhibit cases along the walls, featuring objects from the museum's collection.

After beginning his collecting in his early twenties, Heye (1874–1957) amassed one of the largest private collections of Native American artifacts in the world. The son of a German immigrant who made his fortune in petroleum, Heye first worked as an investment banker. In 1916 he founded the Museum of the American Indian in New York, serving as its director until 1956.

His vast collection, transferred to the Smithsonian in 1989, forms the core of the National Museum of the American Indian. The objects come from virtually all tribes in the United States, as well as from most of those in Canada and a significant number from Central and South America and the Caribbean. The transfer to the Smithsonian brought significant changes to how the collections were stewarded and developed, centering on active partnership with Native peoples. In the years since, the collections have continued to be augmented and diversified, especially in the area of contemporary art. The three buildings that make up the museum, which evolved in a consultative process unique in the Smithsonian's history, provide a rich and sensitive environment for the diverse cultural collections they host.

MUSEUM OF AFRICAN AMERICAN HISTORY AND CULTURE

The National Museum of African American History and Culture (NMAAHC) was dedicated on September 24, 2016, in a moving ceremony featuring then President Barack Obama, who had presided over the groundbreaking in 2012; former President George W. Bush, who had signed the legislation authorizing the building in 2003; and Congressman John Lewis, the civil rights icon who had sponsored a bill to create the museum in 1988 and championed the project for decades.

"Today, a dream too long deferred is a dream no longer," stated Lonnie G. Bunch III, the museum's founding director and now the Smithsonian's fourteenth secretary. The extraordinary building and collections unveiled that day represented the culmination of more than a century of efforts to recognize the contributions of African Americans to American life.

The museum presents a striking profile, with a shimmering, three-tiered crown, the Corona, rising from the grounds adjacent to the Washington Monument on the National Mall. As scholar Mabel O. Wilson explains in her book on the building of the museum, this powerful, inverted form evokes "the joyful gesture of arms raised in praise and celebration." The shape takes inspiration as well from the top portion of a caryatid or architectural column carved by Olowe of Ise (1873–1938), a well-known sculptor among the Yoruba people of West Africa. It denotes both a sense of the sacred and a locus of the transatlantic slave trade. In its unique filigreed sheathing—composed of 3,600 bronze-colored cast aluminum panels—the Corona honors the ornamental metalwork created by enslaved and free African American craftsmen across the South, especially in locales such as Charleston and New Orleans, as well as the unacknowledged labor of countless others who built this nation. The design of the building powerfully embodies the dreams and vision of the museum: inviting contemplation, rewarding close study, holding space for complexity and multilayered histories, and incorporating a vast lexicon of Black traditions from communities all over the United States and the global African diaspora through time.

The three-tiered Corona of the museum (right and opposite) was inspired by a sculpture carved by Olowe of Ise (above). The angle of the tiers is set at the same seventeen-degree angle of the cap of the Washington Monument, a subtle nod to the historic context and the African origins of the obelisk form.

The concept was born of a competition-winning collaboration among three brilliant Black designers: the Tanzanian-born architect Sir David Adjaye (b. 1966) of Adjaye Associates, the late Max Bond (1935–2009) of Davis Brody Bond, and the late Philip Freelon (1953–2019) of the Freelon Group, who together with the construction architecture firm Smith Group JJR formed Freelon Adjaye Bond/Smith (FAB/S). Adjaye served as lead designer; Davis Brody Bond, architects of the mostly subterranean National September 11 Memorial Museum, designed much of the complex programmatic below-ground spaces; and the Freelon Group served as architect of record, with Zena Howard from that firm as senior project manager. A number of other companies and individuals were involved in the design and construction, including women- and minority-led businesses such as McKissack & McKissack.

The significance of the museum's location on the National Mall can hardly be overstated. A museum dedicated to telling a history that has long been suppressed now has pride of place on what is arguably the nation's most important and symbolic public space. Occupying the traditional homelands of the Anacostan or Nacotchtank peoples, the Mall was laid out in the late eighteenth century in a neoclassical plan conceived as a three-dimensional embodiment of democracy. NMAAHC sits at a key juncture of this plan, where the axes connecting the US Capitol and the White House meet, on the grounds of the Washington Monument. Its design skillfully incorporates these and other monuments into its program, using its place on this historic public commons to illuminate stories that help us reach a deeper, more truthful understanding of American history.

Operating within the highly regulated, tradition-bound sphere of DC's monumental core, the architects took care to gesture to the historic setting in elegant and subtle ways. The angle of the Corona tiers is derived from that of the capstone of the neighboring Washington Monument, and the size and layout of the Corona panels take their cue from the bond pattern of the stone obelisk. The symmetry of the museum's form, its height, and its placement engage in an ongoing conversation with its counterpart museums along the Mall. Yet David Adjaye has nevertheless introduced a profoundly innovative architectural creation into the ceremonial landscape of Washington. Its distinctive profile, color, materials, and approach to space distinguish it from its neighbors. For Adjaye, the "black scenography of architectural space can play a counter to the classical, traditional way of making space and offer really creative alternatives."

The facade is entirely wrapped in ornate, patterned panels (opposite), which reflect the light and change in color throughout the day.

The cast aluminum panels covering the exterior were fabricated in a variety of levels of opacity, enabling the museum to regulate the amount of light that enters the building.

Washington, DC, itself is also a part the design. Glass curtain walls on all sides of the columnless entrance hall invite the light and the Mall grounds into the museum (above). As visitors ascend to upper-level galleries through the dazzling perimeter space of the Corona (below), they catch glimpses of the city through the decorative external cladding.

The museum is entered via a dramatic two-hundred-foot-long porch that stretches the length of the south-facing Mall side of the building. The Porch serves as a monumental public version of the domestic front porch common to shotgun houses across the American south, a vital gathering space providing shade, community, and storytelling. NMAAHC's Porch welcomes millions from all over the world, its tapering overhang forming a transition space between interior and exterior. The Porch also stands in dialogue with its fellow museum building entrances along the northern edge of the Mall; its inviting shelter and accessibility offer a notable contrast to the imperial classical temple fronts and grand stairs of the National Museum of Natural History or the National Gallery of Art.

The visitor first encounters Heritage Hall, the vast, columnless central entrance hall. Adjaye conceived it as a new gathering space for the city, and the glass curtain walls on all sides invite the light, the cityscape, and the Mall grounds into the museum. For Mabel O. Wilson, the hall invokes "a metaphorical clearing, the community gathering space of the hush harbor," a secret place used for worship and resistance during slavery.

Nearly 60 percent of the museum is located below grade. An elegant curving stair leads to the capacious, multistory lower Concourse level, where the Sweet Home Café, Oprah Winfrey Theater, Contemplative Court with its Oculus Fountain, and entrance to the History Galleries are located. The History Galleries occupy a colossal exhibition hall built some sixty feet below ground, the largest such space in all the Smithsonian.

These permanent galleries take visitors on an emotional journey spanning the globe, from the fifteenth century to the present day, traversing slavery and freedom, segregation, and an unceasing struggle for liberation and the rights of full citizenship. Via sloping ramps, visitors climb out of the dimmed spaces toward the light as they rise through the centuries. Of the remarkable thirty-five-thousand-item collection amassed over the course of just a decade, two objects—a Jim Crow–era segregated railway car and a prison guard tower from the notorious Angola prison in Louisiana—are so large they had to be installed prior to the completion of the building.

In contrast to the heavy, underground spaces of the History Galleries, the upper-level exhibition galleries are accessed via escalator through the transcendent, dappled light of the Corona perimeter. The surrounding city and its monuments are ever present, glimpsed through the Corona panels and via strategic portals or Lenses. The second floor contains a research center, library, and educational spaces. The third floor holds the Community Galleries, exploring regional stories and African American contributions to civic life through sports, the military, religion, activism, and more. At the crown of the building on the fourth floor are the Culture Galleries, celebrating African American music, visual and performing arts, creativity, and style and tracing their impact in the making of culture both American and global.

An elegant, curving stair connects the entrance hall to the lower Concourse.

Descending by elevator into the cavernous History Galleries, visitors then ascend a series of ramps to experience exhibitions chronicling history from the fifteenth century to today.

The care with which the architectural design is invested with meaning extends as well to the grounds of the museum, the landscaping of which was overseen by Kathryn Gustafson of the design firm Gustafson Guthrie Nichol (GGN). Water is a powerful feature that unites the interior and exterior spaces of the site, as seen especially in the Oculus that connects with the Contemplative Court below. The grounds also play an important role in another key aspect of the museum: its philosophy of sustainable design. The underground galleries extend across much of the site, making the gardens to the north of the museum one of the largest green roofs in the city.

As architect Philip Freelon noted, sustainability resonates deeply with the African American ethos of "making a way out of no way," of reusing and transforming what is at hand. NMAAHC is the Smithsonian's first museum building to achieve a Gold rating from the US Green Building Council's LEED program. The museum boasts many creative passive design strategies. The Porch at the south entrance also features a green roof, and the main roof is covered in photovoltaic solar panels. The upper-level galleries were intentionally nested in an inner core of the Corona, buffering the exhibition spaces from the external building envelope and making it easier and less costly to maintain museum-standard environmental conditions. The natural light that fills much of the building lessens the need for artificial illumination. And the panels of the Corona were designed with varying opacities to let in more light in some places and less in others. Innovative water conservation technologies across the five-acre site save over eight million gallons of city water usage per year.

The architectural design of the National Museum of African American History and Culture connects with intention and care to its environment, inviting the visitor to engage with both the mission of the museum and the city surrounding it. Embracing the message that the museum is for everybody, and that the story that it shares is an essential and fundamentally American story, NMAAHC presents a deeply inspiring, path-setting example of what public architecture and museums can be.

The monumental Porch that welcomes visitors to the museum tilts upward over the reflecting pool on the south plaza, creating a cool and inviting entrance.

At the end of the passage through the History Galleries, visitors discover the Contemplative Court (opposite), centered around a soothing cascade of water. This meditative space is daylit by the dramatic Oculus that projects up into the garden above.

RESEARCH CENTERS

Research is at the core of the Smithsonian's mission as laid out by James Smithson: "the increase and diffusion of knowledge." In addition to the behind-the-scenes areas of the museums, where many laboratories and study centers are located, the institution maintains several research centers, mostly scientific, that are world renowned. Located throughout the Western Hemisphere, these research centers boast buildings as rich and varied as the research that is conducted within.

SMITHSONIAN ASTROPHYSICAL OBSERVATORY

The Smithsonian has been a pioneer in astrophysics for more than a century. As early as 1870, Secretary Joseph Henry expressed a desire to have an observatory on the Smithsonian grounds. His wish was fulfilled by the third secretary, Samuel P. Langley, who established the Smithsonian Astrophysical Observatory in 1890 in a simple wooden shed in the Castle's South Yard. In the observatory's early days, several field stations were set up to augment the facility in Washington. Like the temporary shed behind the Castle, these field stations were small, rudimentary structures, located in isolated areas of Arizona, New Mexico, California, Egypt, Chile, Iran, and South Africa.

The Smithsonian had an early astrophysical solar observation station on the top of Mount Montezuma, Chile (seen here in the mid-twentieth century). Such simple structures were typical of the Smithsonian's early field stations throughout the world.

In 1955 the Smithsonian and Harvard University entered into a partnership, after which the observatory's headquarters were moved to Cambridge, Massachusetts. In 1968 another observatory was opened, on Mount Hopkins, Arizona, today known as the Fred Lawrence Whipple Observatory. An astronomer, Whipple (1906–2004) was the director of the Smithsonian Astrophysical Observatory from 1955 to 1973. The facility named for him represented a radical departure from the traditional observatory design of a telescope located inside an enclosed domed structure. The Whipple Observatory introduced the Multiple Mirror Telescope, a computer-controlled telescope mount with six individual telescopes that functioned as one, greatly increasing the power of observation and setting a new standard for telescope design. This telescope was replaced in 1999 with newer technology, but the building still retains much of its original character.

Close to the summit of the Mauna Kea volcano in Hawaii, 13,386 feet above sea level, is the Submillimeter Array. This complex telescope system is located near Hilo, where the institution constructed an eighteen-thousand-square-foot operations and support facility, designed by Urban Works, Incorporated, of Honolulu, on the grounds of the University of Hawaii. The station features the world's first imaging interferometric telescopic at submillimeter wavelengths, measuring millimeter and submillimeter radiation—the light of colors not visible to the human eye—in order to study the universe in unprecedented detail.

At the Fred Lawrence Whipple Observatory in southern Arizona are the Multiple Mirror Telescope Observatory, a visible-light and infrared telescope (above, top), and the Very Energetic Radiation Imaging Telescope Array System (VERITAS), a set of four telescopes designed to observe gamma rays (above).

Expectations are high for the new Giant Magellan Telescope (GMT), a project of an international consortium of leading universities and science institutions. It is under construction at the Las Campanas Observatory in Chile's Atacama Desert, known for its dark night sky, and scheduled to open in 2029. This telescope, the first of its kind, will have ten times the resolving power of the famous Hubble. The German firm MT Mechatronics is designing the 2,100-ton steel structure, which will hold seven primary mirrors built at the University of Arizona. The GMT mirrors will collect more light than any telescope ever built and will allow for astonishing new discoveries.

Involved in marine science since the late nineteenth century, the Smithsonian is now one of the leaders in the field of biological diversity. Its Tropical Research Institute, a collection of sites located on both coasts and in the middle of the Republic of Panama, developed as an outgrowth of the 1910 Smithsonian Biological Survey of the Panama Canal Zone. This survey of flora and fauna, on land that would be flooded by the creation of the Panama Canal, was one of the earliest environmental impact studies. The architecture here is rich and varied. The buildings—such as the two-story visitors center on Barro Colorado Island, built in the 1920s as the institute's first laboratory—reflect the vernacular of the center's tropical location: louvered windows, verandas, and a mixture of wood and concrete predominate. The simplicity of these buildings' designs belies their functionality in humid climates.

In the 1950s, Adela Gómez and Carl Koford (above) managed what is now the Smithsonian Tropical Research Institute. Today, the Earl S. Tupper Research and Conference Center in Panama City (below) is the heart of the Institute.

When the Canal Zone was returned to Panama under the 1977 treaty with the United States, several former US military buildings were acquired by the institute and converted into offices, exhibit space, and laboratories. The Italianate-style Ancon Building of 1916, originally part of the Gorgas Army Hospital in Panama City's Ancon area, was attached to the hospital's former mortuary and had a fully equipped operating room. "My office for twenty-five years or so," one scientist remarked, "was the chemical lab with drains in the floor."

The institute's administrative center has historically been located in the Earl S. Tupper Research and Conference Center, located on Ancon Hill. The building, which includes a library, a lecture hall, laboratories, and offices, was designed by the Panamanian architect Octavio Méndez Guardia (1918–2011) and dedicated in 1990. It was built on the site of the historic 1906 Tivoli Hotel, where visitors came to view the construction of the Panama Canal. The hotel was demolished in 1975 because of termite infestation, but a small, one-story building once used as a kitchen remains and is in use as offices.

In 2003 the institute opened a new laboratory at its field station Bocas del Toro on Panama's Caribbean coast. Designed in a tropical style by the firm Kiss + Cathcart of Brooklyn, New York, the building champions sustainable design elements. The solar roof, for example, collects rainwater, provides shade, and produces most of the laboratory's electricity.

As the scientific program at STRI has grown, the Smithsonian sought space to consolidate their research facilities. In 2007, STRI purchased land near Gamboa, a town founded in 1916 for the workers of the Panama Canal dredging operation. At the same time, Panama granted STRI custodianship of an additional 155 acres of adjacent forest reserve. The property, ringed by Soberanía National Park and Pipeline Road, and located at the center of the Panama Canal Watershed, saw the inauguration of a major new laboratory building in 2016. The Gamboa Laboratory brings together long-standing terrestrial research on animal behavior, forest ecology, evolution, and climate-change biology. In addition to supporting staff scientists, it welcomes hundreds of scientific visitors from dozens of countries all over the globe, all working to advance groundbreaking research on tropical forests and marine ecosystems.

The facilities at STRI's Gamboa facility, surrounded by the lowland tropical forest of Panama's Soberanía National Park, provide laboratories and housing for visiting scientists.

CARIBBEAN CORAL REEF ECOSYSTEMS PROGRAM

Simple wooden structures in pastel colors fit their tropical location at the Caribbean Coral Reef Ecosystems Program at Carrie Bow Cay, Belize.

This laboratory, located at Carrie Bow Cay on one acre of the Belize Barrier Reef, was established in 1972. A part of the National Museum of Natural History, it serves as a research base for scientists working across the region. The architecture on this small island mirrors its tropical location, with structures integrated among palm trees, white beaches, and the azure sea. Small, pastel-colored colonial-style buildings, with corrugated metal roofs and timber siding, are raised on stilts to allow for water flow and ventilation.

SMITHSONIAN MARINE STATION

Created in 1969, this station in Fort Pierce, Florida, is dedicated to the study of south Florida's ecosystems and biodiversity. It has evolved from its first home on a World War II–vintage floating barge to an eight-acre campus. Its structures for research, storage, and administration are designed in a simple tropical style, like those of the Smithsonian's other tropical facilities.

The Tyson House is a modern version of the tropical vernacular architecture prevalent at the Smithsonian Marine Station. Designed by the Florida architect Peter Jefferson (1928–2015) in 1977 for Peter and Jeanne Tyson, it was relocated from Vero Beach, Florida, to the station in Fort Pierce as a gift from the owners.

Smithsonian Environmental Research Center

Devoted to the study of the connections between atmosphere, watershed, and estuary, and the human impacts on those systems, this center in Edgewater, Maryland, is located on 2,700 acres of land adjacent to the Rhode River, a subestuary of the Chesapeake Bay. Before the property was bequeathed to the Smithsonian in 1964, the land that SERC occupies served as seasonal fishing and hunting grounds for Native Americans, and later for colonial settlers, enslaved people, and farmers. The remains of two tobacco plantations survive at SERC: Sellman House, a mid-nineteenth-century building with a 1735 kitchen wing, built on an earlier foundation; and the ruins of the abandoned Java mansion. This latter property was acquired by SERC in 2007, extending the Smithsonian's capacity to protect undeveloped land in the area. It has also spurred the creation of an archeology lab and intensive environmental archeological investigations, staffed primarily by citizen scientist volunteers. In 2014, SERC opened the Smithsonian's first LEED-Platinum building, the Charles McC. Mathias Laboratory. In partnership with field stations and researchers around the globe, SERC's research has expanded in scale, taking the Chesapeake Bay as a model for studying complex environmental issues facing the world.

The Charles McC. Mathias Laboratory, designed by EwingCole and designated LEED Platinum for energy efficiency and sustainability, features a state-of-the-art, seventy-two-thousand-square-foot laboratory.

Charles McC. Mathias Laboratory

Museum Support Center

With more than 155 million objects and specimens, the Smithsonian's collections are so extensive and diverse that only 2 percent can be displayed to the public at any given time. Objects were originally stored in each museum, but because the collections expanded much more rapidly than the buildings, off-site storage had to be found. One curator at the Natural History Museum devised a plan to draw attention to the overcrowded conditions: in response to his director's request for a specimen to decorate the office, he delivered a stuffed African rhinoceros.

As it planned for expansion in the 1960s, the Smithsonian recognized that the space on the Mall should be dedicated primarily to public access and that research and storage should be located off site. Property was found six miles from the Mall, in Suitland, Maryland, adjacent to the World War II–era Quonset huts of the Paul E. Garber Preservation, Restoration, and Storage Facility of the National Air and Space Museum.

The Smithsonian's innovative Museum Support Center, authorized by Congress in 1975 and opened in 1983, was designed by the Washington, DC, firm Metcalf/Keyes Condon Florance. Covering four and a half acres of land abutting a wooded area, the center is made up of a series of rectangular storage buildings in precast concrete, known as pods. The original 524,000-square-foot, four-pod structure was designed in a zigzag shape to enable additions without compromising the design concept. To protect the different collections, the pods were built with climate control and storage units in all shapes and sizes. Opposite the pods is a smaller building that mirrors the form of the pods and houses offices and research facilities. The support center also serves as the home of the

This panoramic photograph captures some of the National Museum of Natural History's anthropological collections, together with the staff who care for them, in Pod 4.

Smithsonian's pioneering Museum Conservation Institute, the center for research in and conservation of the institution's collections. The two buildings are connected by a covered walkway, which provides two points of access to the complex, one for visitors and one for items in the collection—keeping the objects separate from circulation corridors and adding an additional layer of protection to the site. The center is near the Suitland Parkway, a scenic drive constructed during World War II to connect military installations between what are now Andrews and Bolling Air Force Bases.

In 2007, a fifth pod was opened, covering some 120,000 square feet. Designed by the Philadelphia firm Ewing Cole in keeping with the original pod design, it houses the Natural History Museum's "wet collection" (specimens preserved in alcohol and formalin). The building features the latest technology for the safe use of flammable liquids, to ensure the safety of the largest such collection in the country. Pod 3, the original "wet collection" storage building, was renovated in 2010 to receive the collections of the National Asian Art Museum, National Museum of African Art, and Hirshhorn. A biorepository, with capacity to store over four million cryotubes containing frozen tissue samples, was established in 2011. Pod 6 is currently in design.

A new master plan for the Suitland Collections Center campus as a whole, of which the Museum Support Center forms part, enhances sustainability and envisions a new development of storage modules and support spaces configured in a "necklace" or pinwheel. Over the course of the next forty years, the Smithsonian is projected to add over one million gross square feet on this behind-the-scenes campus.

Serving as both storage facility and conservation laboratory, the Museum Support Center opened in 1983 with four pods. The Bjarke Ingels Group's Master Plan shows the construction of additional storage pods and other building elements. The National Museum of the American Indian's Cultural Resources Center is seen in the upper right.

CHRONOLOGY

The dates given indicate the starting and ending years of design and construction of the museum buildings.

1838–68
Old Patent Office Building (Smithsonian American Art Museum and National Portrait Gallery)

1847–55
The Castle

1859–74
Corcoran Gallery of Art (Renwick Gallery)

1879–81
Arts and Industries Building

1889–present
National Zoo

1890–present
Smithsonian Astrophysical Observatory

1901–3
Andrew Carnegie Mansion (Cooper Hewitt, Smithsonian Design Museum)

1902–7
US Customs House (George Gustav Heye Center, National Museum of the American Indian)

1903–11
National Museum of Natural History

1911–14
City Post Office (National Postal Museum)

1917–23
Freer Gallery of Art

1923–present
Tennenbaum Marine Observatories Network (Tropical Research Institute, Caribbean Coral Reef Ecosystems Program, Marine Station, Environmental Research Center)

1957–64
National Museum of American History

1967–74
Hirshhorn Museum and Sculpture Garden

1974–present
Smithsonian Conservation Biology Institute (National Zoo)

1972–76
National Air and Space Museum

1977–87
The Quadrangle (National Museum of African Art, Arthur M. Sackler Gallery, S. Dillon Ripley Center, Enid A. Haupt Garden)

1983–present
Museum Support Center

1984
Anacostia Community Museum (opened in 1967 at another site)

1995–2004
National Museum of the American Indian, Mall Building

1996–98
Cultural Resources Center, National Museum of the American Indian

2000–2003
Steven F. Udvar-Hazy Center, National Air and Space Museum

2012–16
National Museum of African American History and Culture

DIRECTORY

Anacostia Community
Museum
1901 Fort Place SE
Washington, DC

Arts and Industries Building
900 Jefferson Drive SW
Washington, DC

The Castle
1000 Jefferson Drive SW
Washington, DC

Cooper Hewitt, Smithsonian
Design Museum
2 East Ninety-first Street
New York, New York

Freer Gallery of Art
Twelfth Street and
Jefferson Drive SW
Washington, DC

Hirshhorn Museum and
Sculpture Garden
Independence Avenue at
Seventh Street SW
Washington, DC

Museum Support Center
4210 Silver Hill Road
Suitland, Maryland

National Air and Space
Museum
Sixth Street and
Independence Avenue SW
Washington, DC
including the
Steven F. Udvar-Hazy Center
14390 Air and Space
Museum Parkway
Chantilly, Virginia

National Museum
of African American History
and Culture
1400 Constitution Avenue NW
Washington, DC

National Museum
of American History
Fourteenth Street and
Constitution Avenue NW
Washington, DC

National Museum
of the American Indian
Fourth Street and
Independence Avenue SW
Washington, DC
including the
Cultural Resources Center
4220 Silver Hill Road
Suitland, Maryland
and the
George Gustav Heye Center
One Bowling Green
New York, New York

National Museum
of Natural History
Tenth Street and
Constitution Avenue NW
Washington, DC

National Portrait Gallery
Eighth and F Streets NW
Washington, DC

National Postal Museum
2 Massachusetts Avenue NE
Washington, DC

National Zoo
3001 Connecticut Avenue NW
Washington, DC
including the
Conservation Biology Institute
1500 Remount Road
Front Royal, Virginia

The Quadrangle
*(including the Arthur M. Sackler
Gallery, Enid A. Haupt Garden,
National Museum of African Art,
and S. Dillon Ripley International Center)*
1100 Jefferson Drive SW
Washington, DC

Renwick Gallery of Art
Seventeenth Street and
Pennsylvania Avenue NW
Washington, DC

Smithsonian
American Art Museum
Eighth and F Streets NW
Washington, DC

Smithsonian Institution
Building *(The Castle)*
1000 Jefferson Drive SW
Washington, DC

RESEARCH CENTERS

Caribbean Coral Reef
Ecosystems Program
Carrie Bow Cay, Belize

Smithsonian
Astrophysical Observatory
60 Harvard Street
Cambridge, Massachusetts
*(with facilities in Arizona,
Hawaii, and Chile)*

Smithsonian Environmental
Research Center
647 Contees Wharf Road
Edgewater, Maryland

Smithsonian Marine Station
701 Seaway Drive
Fort Pierce, Florida

Smithsonian Tropical
Research Institute
Luis Clement Avenue
Balboa, Ancon
Republic of Panama

SELECTED BIBLIOGRAPHY

Of the many books and publications about the Smithsonian, the following are just a few. More detailed histories and photographs can be found on the websites of the individual museums, the Smithsonian Libraries and Archives (www.siarchives.si.edu), and the Office of Architectural History and Historic Preservation (www.si.edu/ahhp).

GENERAL

Ewing, Heather. *The Lost World of James Smithson: Science, Revolution, and the Birth of the Smithsonian.* New York: Bloomsbury, 2007.

Lubar, Steven, and Kathleen M. Kendrick. *Legacies: Collecting America's History at the Smithsonian.* Washington, DC: Smithsonian Institution Press, 2001.

Ottesen, Carol. *A Guide to Smithsonian Gardens.* Washington, DC: Smithsonian Books, 2011.

Park, Edwards. *Treasures of the Smithsonian.* Washington, DC: Smithsonian Institution Press, 1983.

Ripley, S. Dillon. *The Sacred Grove.* New York: Simon and Schuster, 1969.

THE MALL

Field, Cynthia R., and Nathan Glazer. *The National Mall: Rethinking Washington's Monumental Core.* Baltimore: Johns Hopkins University Press, 2008.

Longstreth, Richard W., editor. *The Mall in Washington, 1791–1991.* Washington, DC: National Gallery of Art, 1991.

Penczer, Peter R. *The Washington National Mall.* Arlington, VA: Oneonta Press, 2007.

THE CASTLE

Field, Cynthia R., Richard E. Stamm, and Heather P. Ewing. *The Castle: An Illustrated History.* Washington, DC: Smithsonian Institution Press, 1993.

Gibson, Terrica. "'There are whole lots of things I know but I never say anything,' African Americans and the Smithsonian, 1852–1920." Smithsonian Sesquicentennial SI History Lecture Series, February 18, 1996. Unpublished mss., Smithsonian Institution Archives Research Files.

Hafertepe, Kenneth. *America's Castle: The Evolution of the Smithsonian Building and Its Institution, 1840–1878.* Washington, DC: Smithsonian Institution Press, 1984.

Owen, Robert Dale. *Hints on Public Architecture.* New York: Da Capo Press, 1978. Facsimile of 1849 edition.

Peck, Garrett. *The Smithsonian Castle and The Seneca Quarry.* Charleston, SC: The History Press, 2013.

Stamm, Richard E. *The Castle: An Illustrated History (Second Edition).* Washington, DC: Smithsonian Books, 2012.

ARTS AND INDUSTRIES BUILDING

Beauchamp, Tanya Edwards. *From Germany to America: Shaping a Capital City Worthy of a Republic. Historic Preservation Solutions for Adolf Cluss Buildings, 1962–2005.* Washington, DC: Adolf Cluss Exhibition Project, 2005.

Lessoff, Alan, and Christof Mauch, editors. *Adolf Cluss, Architect: From Germany to America.* Oxford, England, and New York: Berghahn, 2005.

NATIONAL
ZOOLOGICAL PARK

Ewing, Heather. "The Architecture of the National Zoological Park," in *New Worlds, New Animals: From Menagerie to Zoological Park in the Nineteenth Century.* Baltimore: Johns Hopkins University Press, 1996.

Ewing, Heather. "An Architectural History of the National Zoological Park." Unpublished manuscript, May 1990. Smithsonian Institution Archives Research Files.

Mergan, Alexa. "From Bison to BioPark: 100 Years of the National Zoo." Washington, DC: Friends of the National Zoo, 1989.

NATIONAL MUSEUM
OF NATURAL HISTORY

Field, Cynthia R., and Jeffrey T. Tilman. "Creating a Model for the National Mall: The Design of the National Museum of Natural History." *Journal of the Society of Architectural Historians,* 63 (March 2004), 52–73.

Yochelson, Ellis. *The Natural History Museum: 75 Years in the New National Museum.* Washington, DC: Smithsonian Institution Press, 1985.

FREER GALLERY OF ART

Lawton, Thomas, and Linda Merrill. *Freer: A Legacy of Art.* Freer Gallery of Art. New York: Harry N. Abrams, 1993.

Morgan, Keith N. *Charles A. Platt: The Artist as Architect.* Architectural History Foundation. Cambridge, MA: MIT Press, 1985.

NATIONAL MUSEUM
OF AMERICAN HISTORY

Cohen, Marilyn Sara. "A First Tentative Step Toward Modernism." *AIA Journal* (1981), 49–53.

Wilson, Richard Guy. "High Noon on the Mall: Modernism versus Traditionalism, 1910–1970." *Studies in the History of Art,* 30 (1991), 142–67.

SMITHSONIAN AMERICAN
ART MUSEUM/NATIONAL
PORTRAIT GALLERY

Evelyn, Douglas. *A Public Building for a New Democracy: The Patent Office Building in the Nineteenth Century.* Ann Arbor, MI: University Microfilms, 1997.

Robertson, Charles J. *Temple of Invention: History of a National Landmark.* Smithsonian Institution. London and New York: Scala Publishers, 2006.

RENWICK GALLERY OF ART

Robertson, Charles J. *American Louvre: A History of the Renwick Gallery Building.* London: D. Giles Limited, 2015.

ANACOSTIA
COMMUNITY MUSEUM

Hutchinson, Louise Daniel. *The Anacostia Story: 1608–1930.* Washington, DC: Smithsonian Institution Press, 1977.

Kinard, Joy G. *The Man, the Movement, the Museum: the Journey of John R. Kinard as the First African American Director of a Smithsonian Institution Museum.* Washington, DC: A.P. Foundation Press, 2017.

HIRSHHORN MUSEUM
AND SCULPTURE GARDEN

Fletcher, Valerie. *A Garden for Art: Outdoor Sculpture at the Hirshhorn Museum.* Washington, DC: Hirshhorn Museum, 1998.

Krinsky, Carol Herselle. *Gordon Bunshaft of Skidmore, Owings & Merrill.* Architectural History Foundation. Cambridge, MA: MIT Press, 1988.

NATIONAL AIR
AND SPACE MUSEUM

Dailey, John R., and John Glenn. *Smithsonian National Air and Space Museum: An Autobiography.* Washington, DC: National Geographic, 2010.

Ezell, Lin. *Building America's Hangar: The Steven F. Udvar-Hazy Center.* Washington, DC: National Air and Space Museum, in association with D. Giles Limited, London, 2004.

Kudalis, Eric. *Gyo Obata.* Minneapolis: Capstone Press, 1966.

McMahon, Michael. "The Romance of Technological Prowess: A Critical Review of the National Air and Space Museum," in *Technology and Culture* (1981).

Obata, Gyo, and Hellmuth Obata and Kassabaum. *Gyo Obata, 1954–1990.* Tokyo: Eando Yu, 1990.

COOPER HEWITT, SMITHSONIAN DESIGN MUSEUM

Dolkart, Andrew S. *Cooper-Hewitt National Design Museum: The Andrew and Louise Carnegie Mansion.* London and New York: Scala Publishers, 2002.

Ewing, Heather. *Life of a Mansion: The Story of Cooper Hewitt, Smithsonian Design Museum.* New York: Cooper Hewitt, Smithsonian Design Museum, 2014.

THE QUADRANGLE

Park, Edwards, and Jean-Paul Carlhian. *A New View from the Castle: Arthur M. Sackler Gallery, National Museum of African Art, S. Dillon Ripley Center, Enid A. Haupt Garden.* Washington, DC: Smithsonian Institution Press, 1987.

NATIONAL MUSEUM OF THE AMERICAN INDIAN

Blue Spruce, Duane (Laguna/Ohkay Owingeh), editor. *Spirit of a Native Place: Building the National Museum of the American Indian.* Washington, DC: National Geographic Press, 2004.

Blue Spruce, Duane (Laguna/Ohkay Owingeh) and Tanya Thrasher (Cherokee), editors. *The Land Has Memory: Indigenous Knowledge, Native Landscapes, and the National Museum of American Indian.* Washington, DC: Smithsonian Books, 2008.

Cardinal, Douglas, and Jeannette Armstrong. *The Native Creative Process.* Penticton, British Columbia: Theytus Books, 1991.

Past, Present, and Future: Challenges of the National Museum of American Indian. Washington, DC: National Museum of American Indian, 2011.

NATIONAL MUSEUM OF AFRICAN AMERICAN HISTORY AND CULTURE

Bunch, Lonnie G., III. *A Fools' Errand: Creating the National Museum of African American History and Culture in the Age of Bush, Obama, and Trump.* Washington, DC: Smithsonian Books, 2019.

Conwill, Kinshasha Holman. "To Reap the Harvest Wonderful: On Sustainability at the National Museum of African American History and Culture." *American Art,* 28:3 (2014), 20–27.

Enwezor, Okwui and Zoë Ryan, editors. *David Adjaye: Form, Heft, Material.* Chicago: Art Institute of Chicago, 2016.

Ruffins, Fath Davis. "Building Homes for Black History: Museum Founders, Founding Directors, and Pioneers, 1915–95." *The Public Historian* (2018): 13–43.

Wilkinson, Michelle Joan. "Not Grandpa's Porch, Or Is It?: Musings on the New Museum on the Mall." *International Review of African American Art,* 25:2 (2015), 52–61.

Wilson, Mabel O. *Begin with the Past: Building the National Museum of African American History & Culture.* Washington, DC: Smithsonian Books, 2016.

SMITHSONIAN RESEARCH CENTERS

Abbott, C. G. *An Account of the Astrophysical Observatory of the Smithsonian Institution, 1904–1953.* Washington, DC: Smithsonian Institution, 1966.

Christen, Catherine A. "At Home in the Field: Smithsonian Tropical Field Stations in the U.S. Panama Canal Zone and the Republic of Panama." *The Americas,* vol. 58, no. 4 (2002), 537–75.

DeVorkin, David H. *Fred Whipple's Empire: The Smithsonian Astrophysical Observatory, 1955–1973.* Washington, DC: Smithsonian Institution Scholarly Press, 2018.

Jones, Bessie Zaban. *Lighthouse of the Skies: The Smithsonian Astrophysical Observatory: Background and History, 1846–1955.* Washington, DC: Smithsonian Institution, 1965.

Royte, Elizabeth. *The Tapir's Morning Bath: Mysteries of the Tropical Rain Forest and the Scientists Who Are Trying to Save Them.* New York: Houghton Mifflin Company, 2001.

ACKNOWLEDGMENTS

The authors thank everyone involved in the first edition of this book and refer you to that edition for a complete listing. The book you hold now would not be possible without them. As with the first edition, we are especially grateful to the Smithsonian Women's Committee and to Smithsonian Facilities for providing the funding necessary to publish this book.

We are extremely grateful to the fourteenth secretary of the Smithsonian, Lonnie G. Bunch III, for the incisive foreword he contributed.

Thank you to Sharon C. Park, associate director of the Office of Architectural History and Historic Preservation, and Carly Bond, historic preservation specialist, for their assistance in locating color photographs and updating building projects since the first edition.

We also thank Rick Stamm, curator of the Smithsonian Castle Collection and the expert on the Castle building, for sharing his expertise and for serving as a reviewer of the text. We are grateful as well for the helpful feedback from two additional readers: Pamela M. Henson, director of the Institutional History Division of Smithsonian Libraries and Archives, and Nancy Bechtol, director of Smithsonian Facilities. Much gratitude as well to Michelle Joan Wilkinson and Duane Blue Spruce for their helpful reads of individual chapters.

We are very grateful for the wonderful photographers throughout the institution. Simply put, without them this book would not exist. Many of the contemporary photographs for the first edition were taken by Eric Long and Ken Rahaim, and are now published here in their original color format. We also recognize the work of Chip Clark, Jesse Cohen, Richard Hofmeister, Matt Flynn, Laurie Minor-Penland, Kim Nielen, John Paulson, Dane Penland, Jeff Ploskanka, Richard Strauss, Hugh Talman, Jeff Tinsley, Rick Vargas, and Jim Wallace.

Many of the photographs in the book are used courtesy of the Smithsonian Libraries and Archives. We are grateful to the staff and encourage readers to explore the incredible collection of historic Smithsonian images online.

Special thanks, lastly, to our wonderful Smithsonian Books liaison, Carolyn Gleason, who got us off to a great start, and especially to Julie Huggins, who brought this book over the finish line during the pandemic. Enormous thanks to our outstanding designer, Robert Wiser, and copyeditor, Joanne Reams, for making this second edition a fitting tribute for the 175th anniversary of the Smithsonian.

Heather Ewing and Amy Ballard

INDEX

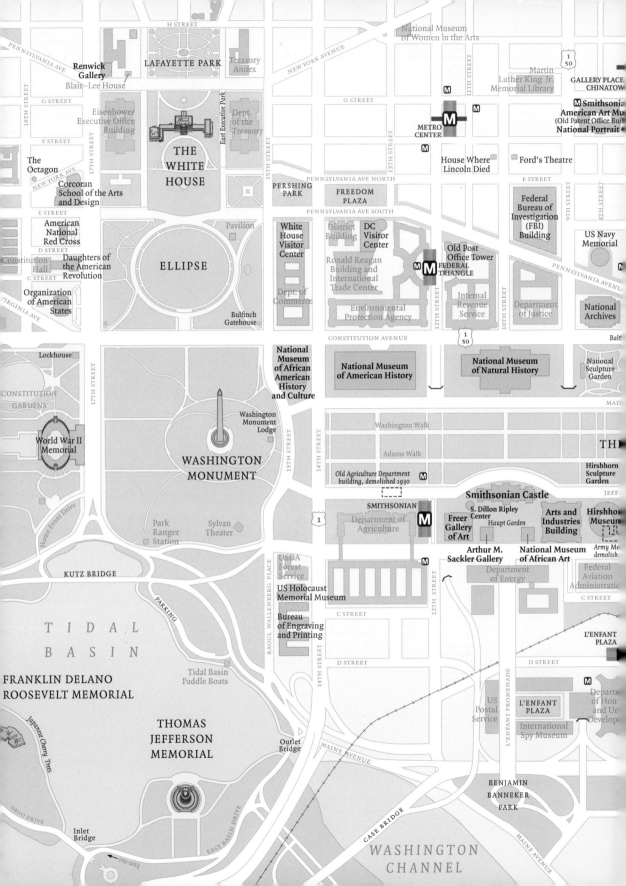